The Hamilton Cookbook

THE
HAMILTON
Cookbook

Cooking, Eating & Entertaining
in Hamilton's World

LAURA KUMIN

A POST HILL PRESS BOOK

The Hamilton Cookbook:
Cooking, Eating, and Entertaining in Hamilton's World
© 2017 by Post Hill Press
All Rights Reserved

ISBN: 978-1-68261-429-7
ISBN (eBook): 978-1-68261-430-3

Interior Design and Composition: Greg Johnson/Textbook Perfect

Post Hill Press
New York • Nashville
posthillpress.com

Published in the United States of America

This book is dedicated to my husband Kevin—
my tireless editor, good natured taste-tester,
and constant support in this
and so many other adventures.

Table of Contents

Acknowledgments

Since the moment I began the research for this book, I have had an incredible support network.

My editor, Debra Englander, made it a pleasure to go from concept to final product. And the folks at Post Hill Press—publisher Anthony Ziccardi and his team of Devon Brown, Billie Brownell, and Sarah Heneghan—have been wonderful all along the way.

The librarians and other staff at the Library of Congress have been amazing. Their expertise, guidance, and help turned my online and in-person trips to the Library into such delightful adventures that I felt a bit guilty calling these forays "work." In particular, I extend my thanks to Arlene Balkansky, Beverly Brannan, Constance Carter, Eric Frazier, Alison Kelly, and Amanda Zimmerman.

The research, cooking, and writing were often done in solitude. But I always had my "crew," keeping me smiling and supporting me. You know who you are, but a few deserve special mention. Heading the list are my husband, Kevin; my kids, Liam and Eleanor; and my mom, Selma. (Funny how my mom never wanted to read a single one of the "too-many-to-count" briefs I wrote as a lawyer, or even the decisions in my biggest cases, but she clamored for multiple copies of this book.) Their encouragement means the world to me.

Many others have helped me along the way too, with advice, a resource suggestion, a hug that energized me, or sometimes all three. I am especially grateful to Arlene Balkansky (who gets double thanks for being a great friend as well as my entrée into the Library of Congress), Vicki Bor, Jamie Butler, Susan Ginsburg, Aviva Goldfarb, Ellen Heiman, Jill Lawrence, John Martin, Jill Phillips, Kate Phillips, Sallie Randolph, Kevin Reeves, Collyn Warner, Monica Adler Werner, and Gail Wides.

Introduction

As a kid, I was a history buff and would have been called a nerd if the word had existed then. I loved fantasizing about what historical figures were really like as people and imagining what it would have been like to live during their times.

I first became fascinated with Alexander Hamilton's world through a book called *George Washington's World*.[1] A 1940s classic, it has captivated generations of young readers because it takes an unusual approach for a history book. While centered on the life of George Washington (Hamilton's friend and mentor), it is much more than a biography. Author Genevieve Foster provides context for Washington's development, accomplishments, and character by providing vignettes about famous people and events that shaped his world. Reading about George Washington's life in the context of his times was a revelation to me. What that book taught me has stayed with me through my entire life, and it has encouraged me to look at historical events and famous people in context, rather than focusing on them in isolation.

There is another aspect to my interest—some might say, obsession—with historical context. When learning about famous people, I'm always fascinated by how they lived. The details of daily living tell you so much about a person. I'll take any detail I can get, whether it's about their families, their taste in books, the phrases they liked to repeat, or most important for this book, the food they ate.

Alexander Hamilton is all the rage these days. His life and accomplishments draw us in. Whether you're a history buff or just like a good story, Hamilton is the central character in a fascinating tale.

Despite the success of the Broadway play *Hamilton*, not everyone knows his story. Chapter 1 provides a summary of his too-brief and often tumultuous life. Using his life as a jumping off point, we will explore what Alexander Hamilton's world was like, with an emphasis on food. The timeline at the end of Chapter 1 puts Hamilton's life in context of the world around him, with each noted event in his life paired with a historical event and a food event or fact from the same year. Chapter 2 provides an overview of life in the 18th century West Indies and Colonial/Post-Independence America, the two places he lived. Chapters 3 and 4 go into more depth on the food, cooking, and dining in Hamilton's world. Chapter 5 offers recipes from Hamilton's time, both in their original format (from cookbooks of that era, except for one from a handwritten note) and in a modern version.

What might it have been like to dine with Hamilton at his own home or in places where we know he ate? What was it like to make meals for Hamilton and his family? What foods might they have eaten and what recipes were popular at the time?

Alexander Hamilton was born in the mid-1750s and was killed in a duel in 1804. His life spanned the colonial era into what is often termed the "early Federalist period." We will call the roughly 50-year span of his life "Hamilton's era" or "Hamilton's time" for purposes of defining the period covered by our journey.

We do not know a lot about what Hamilton actually ate. While he wrote lengthy pamphlets and essays about current events, economics, law, and politics and he corresponded at length with friends and family, he didn't seem to pay much attention in his writing to food.[2]

However, we do have descriptions of meals he ate as a guest, particularly when the dinner became part of American history. For example, we know what George Washington and Thomas Jefferson served at dinners to which they invited Hamilton (see Chapter 4). We also know enough about his family and where he lived to understand what dishes he likely ate and how they would have been prepared.

With a bit of imagination and the culinary equivalent of dramatic license, we will journey back to Hamilton's era to learn about, and taste, dishes that range from simple breakfast foods to main courses at dinner and lovely sweets to end a meal.

These recipes in their original form are excerpted from cookbooks popular during Hamilton's time. The modernized versions of those recipes bring the dish into the twenty-first century, using modern language, ingredients, proportions, and kitchen equipment.

Chapter 1

Alexander Hamilton: Who Was He?

Portrait of Alexander Hamilton by John Trumbull

Alexander Hamilton was undoubtedly an extraordinary man; he was also an extraordinarily complicated man.[3] His accomplishments are so many and varied that it is hard to believe that one man did all that he did in 49 years. He wrote poetry, reams of essays and other papers on political philosophy and economic theory, and he published political pamphlets and voluminous reports on the inner workings of government. A military hero and strategist, he was a talented lawyer who argued in front of the Supreme Court, and he created our financial system that has lasted for hundreds of years. He called for the establishment of a military college (West Point), ran a government department, was a trustee of a college that he left without graduating, and wrote *The Federalist Papers*, the pre-eminent exposition on the U.S. Constitution. All this while also being a devoted family man and maintaining friendships in an age when communication meant talking directly in person or writing a letter in longhand.

Yet Hamilton was flawed and inconsistent. He railed against slavery while benefitting from it, and claimed to be against duels while participating in them. He remained married to the same woman and professed great love for her, yet he deceived her and engaged in a torrid, long-term affair with a younger woman.

The Early Years

Hamilton's early life would bring tears to the eyes of even the most hard-hearted reader.

His mother, Rachel Faucette, was of French Huguenot and British ancestry. At the age of sixteen, while living on the island of St. Croix, she married a Dane named Johann Michael Lavien. At least twelve years older than Rachel and apparently not a pleasant man (to put it mildly), Lavien had her thrown in prison after she refused to continue living with him. In 1750, after Rachel was released from prison, she fled to St. Kitts, a nearby island settled by the French and English, leaving her husband with their infant son.

On St. Kitts, Rachel, then in her early twenties, met James Hamilton, a thirty-something Scotsman who had arrived on the island about ten years prior. In short order they had two sons, James Jr. in 1753 and Alexander in 1755.[4] Rachel was still married to Lavien during those years, so the boys were illegitimate.

After James got a new job on St. Croix and the family moved there, he abandoned them when

Birthplace of Alexander Hamilton, Nevis, West Indies

Alexander Hamilton was about ten years old. Hamilton never saw his father again, although later Hamilton wrote to his father and regularly sent him money. As an adult, Hamilton even urged his father, unsuccessfully, to move to the United States.

Rachel Hamilton managed as a single parent by running a grocery store, living above it with her two boys. However, less than 18 months after she settled into life as a shopkeeper, Rachel and Alexander both became horribly sick, and Rachel died. Their sickness and her death were made worse by the medical "cures" of the day which included emetics, medicinal herbs to help a patient emit gas, enemas, and bloodletting. Rachel had few possessions and even those did not go to the orphaned Hamilton boys after Lavien swooped in to claim them for the son she had left behind with him.

The two penniless, pre-teen boys ended up in the care of their uncle-by-marriage, a widower named Peter Lytton. (Peter's wife, Rachel's older sister, had died before Rachel.) Less than two years after Rachel's death, Peter Lytton died too, apparently, a suicide. He left them nothing and Peter's own father, who tried to help the boys, died a short time later. At this point, the brothers parted ways; James Jr. was apprenticed to a carpenter and Alexander, who had already begun to clerk in a trading house, left to live with the family of a merchant named Thomas Stevens. Hamilton formed a lifelong friendship with one of the Stevens's five children,

Edward, who later became a physician and who, in 1793, saved the lives of Hamilton and his wife during a yellow fever epidemic.

Why would a respected family take in a poor boy left alone in the world? And why take in one brother and not the other? Hamilton's biographer Ron Chernow speculates that Hamilton might have been Thomas Stevens's illegitimate son. Chernow found evidence of this possibility, including descriptions of a rather startling resemblance between Hamilton and his friend Edward Stevens. In any case, this turn of events was a lucky break for Alexander Hamilton.

Without family, funds, or formal education, Hamilton was truly a self-made man. A voracious reader even before his mother died, he continued to read prodigiously throughout his life. Hamilton learned French well enough that native French speakers complimented him. When it came to business matters, he was also a quick study. As a clerk at a trading house, Hamilton learned how to trade the local crops, sugar, molasses and rum, for timber, flour, and other supplies. When the head of the firm became ill and could not work for a period, he left Hamilton, still a teenager, in charge. Hamilton also began to write at that time. Beginning with poetry and then moving to a first-person account of a hurricane that struck St. Croix, Hamilton caught the eye of local power brokers when his writings were published in the local paper. That attention served him well, as in 1773 they took up a collection to fund his travel to the American colonies so that he could attend college.

Hamilton's Move to the American Colonies

Once Hamilton arrived in the American colonies, he began his formal studies with energy and impatience. After a short time at a preparatory academy in New Jersey, Hamilton sought admissions acceptance to Princeton. When the school would not agree to accelerate his studies to suit him, Hamilton instead went to King's College (which later became Columbia University). Hamilton intended to become a physician, but he became drawn to debating and political pursuits. In fact, he never graduated from college because the Revolutionary War intervened. After the war, he "read" the law instead of attending law school, learning the requisite materials on his own rather than through a formal school program. At both his undergraduate and law studies, Hamilton pursued an accelerated schedule. In the case of his law studies, Hamilton did the required work to pass the bar in about a year instead of the typical three years.

While at King's College, Hamilton became a Patriot activist. He wrote, spoke, and took part in paramilitary actions in support of the Patriot cause. But perhaps even more notable was his action stopping an angry mob of Patriot students from attacking a teacher with Loyalist (British) sympathies. In that incident, saving the teacher even

though he disagreed with his politics, Hamilton showed the physical and moral courage that would become a hallmark of his later years.

The Revolutionary War Years

At age twenty-one, Hamilton left King's College (without graduating) and joined the Continental Army as an artillery captain. He was popular among his men, sharing their hardships, treating them respectfully, and staying cool under stressful combat conditions.

Once General Washington learned of Hamilton's leadership skills and other talents first-hand during the retreat from New York across New Jersey to Pennsylvania, he promoted Hamilton to his own staff and made him a lieutenant colonel. In 1777, Hamilton began a mentor/friendship relationship with Washington that was to last until Washington's death in 1799. Hamilton was Washington's trusted aide, who spoke for him with authority and whom Washington trusted to write letters and communicate directly with others on Washington's behalf. While their personalities were not always compatible (at one point Hamilton was so disgruntled that he left Washington's staff), Washington remained a source of support for Hamilton throughout the next twenty-two years. At crucial moments when others doubted Hamilton or stood in his path, Washington stayed calmly by his side.

During the Revolutionary War, Hamilton distinguished himself in battle and remained with

Portrait of Elizabeth Schuyler Hamilton

enjoyed the social aspects of his military service. Martha Washington witnessed Hamilton's charm first-hand when she entertained the officers on behalf of her husband.

Hamilton's future wife, twenty-two-year-old Elizabeth Schuyler, came on the scene when she arrived in Morristown to live with her aunt and uncle, Washington's personal physician. Within just a few months, Hamilton and Elizabeth, whom he called Eliza or Betsey, decided to marry.

Elizabeth came from a large, well-to-do and prominent family with strong roots to the Dutch community in Albany, New York. (Her parents both came from wealthy families and her mother was a Van Rennselaer.) Hamilton liked the Schuyler family and found that it provided him entrée into political and social circles throughout his life. Elizabeth did not have formal schooling. Contemporaneous accounts describe her energy and sparkling eyes but she was not considered a great beauty.

Alexander and Elizabeth married at the Schuyler home in 1780 when he was twenty-five and she was twenty-three. Hamilton had no family and only one friend in attendance at the small wedding.

The Hamiltons returned to the Schuyler home in Albany frequently throughout their marriage. Sometimes together, other times individually or accompanied by some or all of their children, Alexander and Elizabeth spent weeks, months, and, in one case, two years living at the mansion with Elizabeth's family.

Washington during the grueling winters at Valley Forge and Morristown, NJ. Even when the conditions were difficult, officers had living arrangements that seem odd to our modern sensibilities. For example, during the war in the winter of 1779–1780, Martha Washington lived near Morristown, NJ, and Hamilton and other officers were treated to receptions and fancy dress balls featuring young women from nearby who came to socialize with them. Hamilton was known as a flirt, and he clearly

Photograph of the drawing room of the Schuyler mansion, Albany, NY

After a short honeymoon, Hamilton returned to the war. Elizabeth soon followed and they lived in New Windsor, New York, where Elizabeth helped Martha Washington entertain the troops. Hamilton left Washington's staff, disgruntled with his position there, but he remained in the military and personally close to Washington until the latter's death in 1799, almost twenty years later. Hamilton served in the Continental Army throughout the rest of the Revolutionary War, and was leading troops at Yorktown when Cornwallis surrendered to General Washington in October 1781.

The Post-War Period

The Hamilton family moved back to Albany for two years after the war ended and their first child, Philip, was born there. Alexander Hamilton became a lawyer, writing his own 177-page, 38-topic study guide for the bar examination that was so impressive, others used it as their own study guide for years afterward. After joining the bar, he opened a law practice in Albany and wrote essays on economics, trade, and taxation on the side.

Hamilton soon became a delegate to the Congress of the Confederation in Philadelphia, the governing body of the United States after the states ratified the Articles of Confederation and before the Constitution created Congress and our current form of government.

In 1783, Hamilton moved his family to lower Manhattan where they lived for a number of years. Hamilton's professional life must have seemed a veritable whirlwind. He participated in politics (including being a delegate to the Constitutional Convention in 1787), practiced law, founded the Bank of New York, and created and wrote the majority of *The Federalist Papers*.

The sheer magnitude of how much Hamilton wrote and the speed at which he did, is staggering. Hamilton authored fifty-two of the eighty-five essays that comprise that seminal explanation of the United States Constitution. He wrote twenty-one of these essays in a two-month period and on two different occasions, he wrote five of the essays within a week.

Hamilton: Husband, Father, and Friend

When he conceived and wrote *The Federalist Papers*, Hamilton was thirty-two years old. He had three children and a fourth on the way, and was working as a lawyer to support his growing family.

Serious, even single-minded when it came to his professional life, Hamilton was warm and tender toward his family. He enjoyed playing music with his daughter Angelica and gave advice on studying to his oldest son, Philip. Following up on his early interest in medicine, he often gave medical advice to Elizabeth on how to care for the children when they became sick. As their family grew, Elizabeth would take the younger children to Albany and leave the older ones with Alexander. Letters to Elizabeth reveal a devoted and demonstrably affectionate husband.

The Hamilton family must have been an active and rather boisterous household. In all, Alexander and Elizabeth had eight children in twenty years. On top of that, they took in other children who needed a home. In one case, the daughter of a fellow King's College graduate and Revolutionary War veteran stayed with the Hamiltons for ten years after her mother died and her father fell on hard times. In another example, they took in the Marquis de Lafayette's son while his father was imprisoned after the French Revolution. Although Elizabeth certainly shouldered the bulk of the family responsibilities,

Hamilton also participated in the care of the family, in normal times and when sickness struck. For example, he nursed his oldest son Philip back to health after Philip almost died of a fever in 1798.

Hamilton had many friends of varied backgrounds. He kept up his friendship with Edward Stevens, from the family who took him in on St. Croix, and made new friends in New York, including an Irish tailor named Hercules Mulligan, who became a spy for the Patriot cause during the Revolutionary War, as well as fellow students at King's College. During the War, he befriended the Marquis de Lafayette and a number of others with whom he served.

In the military he met John Laurens, the son of a wealthy South Carolinian, who died tragically at the end of the Revolutionary War, barely five years after their friendship began. His friendship with Laurens was particularly close, and they exchanged letters that have a frank and intimate tone. Both men developed a deep friendship with the Marquis de Lafayette. Historians and Hamilton biographers have wondered about the true nature of several of Hamilton's relationships, including those with Laurens and Lafayette. But there is no definitive evidence that those men were anything other than close friends.

Another of Hamilton's relationships that has drawn scrutiny is that with his wife's sister, Angelica Schuyler Church. One year older than her sister Elizabeth, Angelica had already eloped with Englishman John Church before Hamilton met Elizabeth. The Churches were quite wealthy and spent a number of years living in Europe. At one point, John Church named Alexander Hamilton as his business agent in the United States.

Angelica Church and Alexander Hamilton were close, exchanging frequent chatty and even flirtatious letters, and visiting whenever they had the chance. Although some have speculated that the relationship was more than friendship, it does not appear that neither John Church nor Elizabeth Hamilton was concerned about the relationship between Angelica and Alexander. Indeed, not only were Angelica and her sister Elizabeth close, John Church and Alexander Hamilton did business together. In fact, John Church and Alexander Hamilton brokered a business deal with (ironically) Aaron Burr—a deal that ended badly. As a result, Burr and Church dueled in 1799, five years before the Burr/Hamilton duel, but they did not injure each other.

Hamilton had a reputation for being charming in social settings and both Alexander and Elizabeth enjoyed entertaining. Ron Chernow, author of an extensively researched Hamilton biography, describes their home as "elegant but unostentatious." As hosts, they would have used the gold embossed porcelain tableware that they had received as a gift from the wealthy Churches. They also relished going to the theater and being guests at teas and fancy parties at the homes of the Washingtons; John Jay and his wife, the Binghams of Philadelphia; and others.

Hamilton and Slavery

Hamilton's relationship to slavery was by no means straightforward. Growing up in the West Indies, he must have seen the incredible brutality and cruelty of the slave system up close. But even his very poor mother owned slaves. When he went to college, some of his fellow students, notably George Washington's stepson, Jacky Custis, brought household slaves with them to school. Unlike Washington and Jefferson, Hamilton did not hold racist views, expressing the belief that "their [black people's] faculties are as good as ours."[5]

When Hamilton was barely thirty years old, he was part of a small group that founded the New York Society for Promoting the Manumission of Slaves. That group campaigned against slavery and promoted its gradual elimination. At the same time, throughout his life, Hamilton was the beneficiary of slave labor in direct and personal ways that must have been apparent to him. His inlaws, the Schuylers, certainly owned slaves, as did his sister and brother-in-law, Angelica and John Church. So too did the Washingtons, Jefferson, and probably everyone else in Hamilton's social circle. He ate meals prepared by slaves and lived in an environment and an economy made possible only by slave labor, even in New York City.

The evidence as to whether the Hamilton family owned slaves is unclear, though Chernow speculates that they may have had one or two household slaves. In any event, Hamilton personally arranged transactions involving the purchase of slaves for the Churches. Regardless of his views on racial equality and efforts to eliminate slavery, Hamilton condoned it and enjoyed the benefits of the slave system.

Hamilton Serving the United States of America

Within months of becoming the first President of the United States, George Washington established the Treasury Department and named Alexander Hamilton as its head. Hamilton is well known for the visionary approach he took in creating the federal economic structure that exists even today. His administrative skills may be less recognized, but they were crucial to the success of the early years of the federal economic system. Hamilton took charge of the details of federal finances and operated the Treasury Department from 1789 to 1795 with incredible energy and attention to detail.

The Reynolds Affair

While he served as Secretary of the Treasury (when he was in his mid- to late thirties), Hamilton and his family lived in Philadelphia, on what is now Walnut Street, near his offices at the Treasury Department. During that time, he had an affair with 23-year-old Maria Reynolds. Hamilton carried on the affair even at his own home, and deceived his wife so that she would not find out about it. The affair lasted about 18 months and, not surprisingly, the cover-up turned out to be much worse than the "crime." Reynolds' husband and a friend of Reynolds blackmailed Hamilton; at some point, Maria joined the conspiracy to extort money from Hamilton to keep the affair quiet. Once Hamilton's political enemies heard of the affair and cover-up, they accused Hamilton of using his government office as Secretary of the Treasury in connection with the hush money payments. (Those who sought to take advantage of Hamilton's dalliance included James Madison, his former friend and fellow *Federalist Papers* essayist.) Hamilton did not deny the affair or the payments once they became known, but he adamantly insisted that it was purely a private indiscretion and that he had never abused the public trust. The affair haunted him, particularly as it become fodder for his enemies even years later. Through it all, Elizabeth stood by him. When the sordid tale became known, Hamilton seemed contrite and more attentive to both his wife and his growing family.

Hamilton's Last Years

By 1795, Hamilton realized that he needed to leave government service and return to a private law practice to support his family. He had spent most of his twenties in the army earning little and, of course, he had no family inheritance. In addition, his

Drawing of The Grange by OH.F. Langman

investments could not provide his family a financial cushion. As Secretary of the Treasury Hamilton earned $3,500 a year (less than $100,000 in current dollars and perhaps as little as $64,000), and he had borrowed money both from his old friend Robert Troup and his brother-in-law John Church to make ends meet. As a lawyer he did well but was not always concerned with collecting his fees.

Although Hamilton returned to his law practice to provide for his family, he did not manage to save money during the years after he left the Treasury Department. To a significant extent, his inability to build a nest egg at that time was due to yet another period of government service. He accepted another military appointment, this time to help put down rebellions against federal taxes, which he had championed.[6] Then, after he returned to private life, Hamilton went into debt in the first years of the 19th century building a new home, called The Grange, in what is now Harlem, NY. When Hamilton died in 1804, he left Elizabeth and their children destitute.

The Grange interior, looking into the dining room

The last few years of Alexander Hamilton's life were, like his beginnings, filled with personal tragedy. In 1801, his oldest child, Philip, died in a duel in Weehawken, the same location where Hamilton would later duel with Aaron Burr. Philip had agreed to the duel to defend his father's honor and died when, at his father's suggestion, he did not shoot his challenger. The death not only devastated Hamilton and his wife, it caused their second child, Angelica, to suffer a mental breakdown from which she never recovered. Two years after Philip's death,

the Hamiltons had their eighth child, a boy named Philip after his older brother. A year later, in 1803, Elizabeth's mother died suddenly.

Hamilton's own death, in the famous 1804 duel with Aaron Burr, was the result of a long-simmering feud between the two men. They had known each other for decades and had even served as co-counsel in a recent high-profile murder case. Yet they disliked each other and had plotted against each other in various political arenas for years. Burr challenged Hamilton to a duel over relatively inconsequential comments Hamilton allegedly had made about Burr's character. Hamilton did not aim his only shot at Burr, while Burr shot Hamilton in the lower abdomen. The next day Hamilton died in New York City with his wife Elizabeth by his side. He left her with debts, seven children (the youngest of whom was two), and no visible means of support. Her father died just a few months later. Elizabeth lived to be ninety-seven years old and spent much of the remaining fifty years of her life working for widows and orphans and to preserve her husband's memory and legacy.

Following is a chronology of Alexander Hamilton's life, along with contemporaneous historical events and food facts:

Timeline of Alexander Hamilton's Life

Year	Hamilton's Age	Event
		In History
		In Food
		In Hamilton's Life
Early 1750s		**King's College Founded (later Columbia University) — 1754**
		Benjamin Thompson (later Count von Rumford) is born. He invented the Rumford fireplace (a precursor to the modern stove), the percolator, and a double boiler. He also introduced the potato as a staple food in Central Europe (1753).
		Hamilton's parents, Rachel & James, meet in St. Kitts, British West Indies. Their son James Jr. (Alexander's older brother) is born in 1753.
1755		**The first steam engine is installed in America. The engine, installed in a copper mine owned by one of Elizabeth Schuyler Hamilton's relatives, pumps water from the mine.**
		Oliver Evans, the inventor of the first automatic flour mill, is born in Delaware.
		Alexander Hamilton is born in St. Kitts, Britsh West Indies.
1765	9 years old	**Britain enacts the Stamp Act, the first direct British tax on the colonists, and the Quartering Act, requiring colonists to temporarily house British soldiers.**
		Tradition says that the first modern restaurant is created by a M. Boulanger in Paris. (This has since been debunked, but remains a popular tale.)
		Hamilton, his mother, & older brother move to Christiansted on St. Croix, where his father had a new job.

Year	Hamilton's Age	Event
1766	10 years old	**After months of protest by the American colonists, Britain repeals the Stamp Act. Despite the repeal, the Act has galvanized the Americans and is credited as being one of the forces that set them on the path toward revolution.**
		On a political mission in London, Benjamin Franklin writes *Further Defense of Indian Corn* for a British newspaper. While ostensibly about corn, the article is really a jibe at the British and their views of the Americans and the Scots.
		Hamilton's father, James, deserts his family & leaves St. Croix. Hamilton never sees him again.
1767–1768	11–13 years old	**Charles Mason and Jeremiah Dixon finished their three year-long survey that would later establish the Mason-Dixon line, separating the North and South during the Civil War.**
		Dr. Joseph Priestly, a theologian and chemist, (among the discoverers of oxygen and also a friend of Benjamin Franklin), creates the first drinkable glass of manmade soda or carbonated water.
		Hamilton's mother, Rachel, dies in 1767. Hamilton & his brother become wards of their cousin, Peter Lytton. Hamilton begins to clerk for the trading firm of Beekman & Cruger during this period (exact year uncertain).
1769	14 years old	**Daniel Boone begins to explore the area that will become Kentucky.**
		The first modern recipe for macaroni and cheese is published in Elizabeth Raffald's *The Experienced French Housekeeper.*
		Hamilton's guardians, Peter Lytton and his father, James die. Hamilton goes to live with merchant Thomas Stevens & his family, while his brother is apprenticed to a tradesman.

Year	Hamilton's Age	Event
1771	16 years old	**In 1769 about 3,000 people were killed after 200,000+ pounds of gunpowder stored in a church basement ignited when lightning struck the church. The British Parliament convenes a committee to investigate and recommend protections against such lightning strikes on gunpowder storage sites. Committee members include Benjamin Franklin.**
		The Connecticut General Assembly reimburses Ezekial Williams for ingredients for Election Day Cake (a variation of a classic English fruitcake), marking the first time that the cake is recorded as being made to celebrate this holiday, second only to Thanksgiving in importance in New England.
		While the head of the firm is on medical leave, Hamilton is left in charge of Beekman & Cruger. In April 1771, Hamilton publishes poetry in the local paper.
1772	17 years old	**Colonists in Rhode Island set fire to the British navy ship Gaspee, sent to enforce maritime laws and prevent smuggling. The burning is a significant event in the lead up to the American Revolution.**
		Potatoes had been illegal to grow and consume in France since 1748, because they were believed to be poisonous. Some even claimed that they caused leprosy. Due to the efforts of a French medical army officer who ate potatoes for many years as a prisoner of war during the Seven Years War, potatoes are finally made legal in France.
		Hamilton publishes his first major piece of writing, an account of a hurricane that struck St. Croix.
1773–1774	18–19 years old	**The Boston Tea Party takes place in Boston Harbor (in 1773).**
		Johnny Appleseed (John Chapman) is born in Massachusetts.
		Hamilton goes to the American colonies and enrolls in King's College (later Columbia University.) On July 6, 1774, he speaks at a mass meeting, endorsing the Boston Tea Party, condemning British taxation policies in the colonies & endorsing a boycott of British goods.

Year	Hamilton's Age	Event
1775	20 years old	**Battle of Lexington and Concord is fought on April 15. George Washington is named Commander-in-Chief in June and two days later, the Battle of Bunker Hill occurs.**
		The Massachusetts Provincial Council sets the daily ration for soldiers as follows: 1 pound of bread, ½ pound of beef and ½ pound of pork; and if pork cannot be had, then 1 ¼ pounds of beef; and one day in seven they shall have 1 ¼ pound of salt fish, instead of one day's allowance of meat; 1 pint of milk, or if milk cannot be had, ½ cup of rice, 1 quart of good spruce or malt beer, ½ cup of peas or beans, or other sauce equivalent, plus 6 ounces of good butter per week.
		After Lexington and Concord, Hamilton joins other men in taking arms from British soldiers & forming an ad hoc military company in New York City.
1776	21 years old	**The Declaration of Independence is signed on July 4th.**
		There are 12 bakeries in New York.
		After participating in several skirmishes, Hamilton is named an artillery captain in charge of a regiment he and a friend form. After the British shell New York, he is part of the force under Washington that retreats across New Jersey to Pennsylvania.
1777	22 years old	**The Articles of Confederation are signed in November.**
		During the early winter at Valley Forge, food is scarce for the soldiers and much of their nourishment comes from "firecake," flour and water cooked over an open fire.
		Washington invites Hamilton to join his staff as an aide-de-camp. After the Articles of Confederation are signed and sent to states for ratification, Hamilton criticizes them for failing to give Congress taxing power.

Year	Hamilton's Age	Event
1778	23 years old	**Captain James Cook lands on the Hawaiian Islands.**
		In February, Congress orders that bakers be enlisted into the army consisting of a director to be paid $50 per month and 3 rations, 3 sub-directors at $40 & 2 rations, 12 foremen at $30 & 1 ration & 64 bakers at $24 & 1 ration.
		After falling gravely ill, Hamilton recovers, then rejoins Washington at Valley Forge. Hamilton participates in his first duel, as a second for his good friend John Laurens. The duel results in injury, but no deaths.
1779–1780	24–25 years old	**After betraying the colonies, Benedict Arnold joins the British. The deadliest Atlantic hurricane on record kills 20,000-30,000 people in the Carribbean. Among those who die from the hurricane are 4,000 French soldiers headed for the U.S. when their 40 ships capsize off Martinique.**
		The winter of 1780 is so harsh in Morristown and the soldiers so desperate that one private reports seeing a soldier roast and eat shoes, and reports hearing that some of the officers killed aand ate a dog.
		Elizabeth Schuyler arrives at Morristown in February. Before the end of March, she and Hamilton decide to wed. While working on military matters during the day, Hamilton writes a 7,000-word letter to a member of the Continental Congress from New York containing a critique of the Articles of Confederation and visionary plans for the powers of the executive and legislative branches of the federal government.
1781	26 years old	**The Continental Congress adopts the Articles of Confederation. The Revolutionary War ends in October, with Cornwallis' surrender to Washington at Yorktown.**
		Wheat is selling for 7–8 shillings ($2.34 to $2.68) per bushel in New England; oats for 2 shillings 8 pence (89 cents); rye for 4–5 shillings ($1.34 to $1.67) and Indian corn for 4 shillings ($1.34) per bushel.
		Hamilton leaves Washington's staff after a tense confrontation. He continues to serve in the army as commander of a NY Light Infantry Battalion.

Year	Hamilton's Age	Event
1782	27 years old	**The Bank of North America, the first commercial bank in the U.S. is federally chartered in Philadelphia.**
		Antoine Beauvilliers opens what is purported to be the first "real" restaurant in Paris. He becomes a famous restauranteur and author of an important French cookbook, *l'Art du Cuisinier* translated into English under the title *The Art of French Cookery*.
		The Hamiltons' first child, Philip, is born and the family moves in with her parents for 2 years. Hamilton does accelerated study for the bar and opens up a law practice in Albany, as does Aaron Burr at about the same time. He becomes the receiver of continental taxes for New York and soon after goes to Philadelphia to participate in the Confederation Congress.
1783	28 years old	**The Revolutionary War fighting ends and General Washington orders the Continental Army disbanded. Twenty-seven year old Mozart's symphony #36 premieres in Linz, Austria.**
		Frederic Tudor, "the Ice King," is born. He pioneered the export of block ice, cut from frozen New England pond in the winter and shipped to the Caribbean and Europe, where it is stored in insulated warehouses.
		Elizabeth's sister Angelica Schuyler Church, her husband John and their children leave for Europe. John Church, names Hamilton as the former's business agent in the U.S., which consumes much of Hamilton's time. The Hamiltons move to a home on Wall St. in lower Manhattan.
1784	29 years old	**The U.S. Congress of the Confederation ratifies the Treaty of Paris, officially ending the Revolutionary War.**
		Twenty-nine year old Oliver Evan's automatic flour mill goes into operation near Philadelphia. The mill moves grain automatically through a series of five machines on a production line and delivers flour at the end, packed in barrels.
		Hamilton founds the Bank of New York while practicing law in New York City. The Hamiltons' second child, Angelica, is born in September.

Year	Hamilton's Age	Event
1785	30 years old	**Samuel Ellis advertises to sell Oyster (Ellis) Island, but gets no takers. Napoleon Bonaparte graduates from the military academy in Paris.**
		A British inventor patents the beer-pump handle.
		Hamilton and a small group found the anti-slavery group, The New York Society for Promoting the Manumission of Slaves.
1786	31 years old	**The U.S. Congress adopts the silver dollar and the decimal system of currency.**
		Commercially made ice cream is first advertised .
		Hamilton is elected to the New York legislature and then to the Annapolis convention. At the convention, the delegates issue a report Hamilton writes calling on the country to establish a strong federal government. The Hamiltons' third child, Alexander, is born in May.
1787–1788	32–33 years old	**The U.S. Constitution is drafted and ratified by enough states that it becomes effective. New York City becomes the first capital of the U.S.**
		Hannah Glasse's *The Art of Cookery Made Plain & Easy* is published.
		Hamilton is a delegate to the Constitutional Convention. He also creates, supervises, and writes 55 of the 85 essays (John Jay and James Madison write the remainder) that constitute The Federalist Papers. *The essays, urging ratification of the Constitution, are now considered perhaps the foremost source for understanding the original intent of the Constitution's drafters. The Hamiltons' fourth child, James Alexander, is born in April, 1788.*

Year	Hamilton's Age	Event
1789	34 years old	**George Washington is sworn in as the first U.S. President in April and the French Revolution begins with the storming of the Bastille on July 14th (now celebrated as Bastille Day)**
		It is widely reported that the Hamiltons served George Washington ice cream at a dinner on June 13, which appears to have been Washington's introduction to the sweet confection.
		A week after creating the Treasury Department, Washington appoints Hamilton as Secretary of the Treasury.
1790	35 years old	**George Washington delivers the first State of the Union Address, the Supreme Court convenes for the first time (in New York), the U.S. Congress moves from New York City to Philadelphia and passes the Assumption Bill (promoted by Hamilton) to make the federal government responsible for state debts.**
		The first US patent is granted. It is for a process that produced, among other things, pearlash, used in baking to produce quick rise breads. (Baking powder does not become available until the mid-1800s.)
		Hamilton submits his "First Report on the Public Credit," arguing for federal assumption of state debts. Jefferson hosts a dinner for Madison and Hamilton at which the three men hammer out a compromise that implements Hamilton's plan for federal assumption, and Hamilton agrees to encourage his fellow northerners to accept the creation of the capital in the South, along the Potomac River.

Year	Hamilton's Age	Event
1791–1792	36–37 years old	**In December 1791, the U.S. adopts the Bill of Rights, the first 10 amendments to the Constitution. In 1792, Washington is elected to his second term as President and Congress establishes the U.S Mint. In France, the Revolution continues; the revolutionary forces capture Louis XVI and his family trying to escape. Mozart's *The Magic Flute* premieres in Vienna.**
		Patents are issued in the US for the manufacture of gelatin and for a machine that threshes corn and grain. (Threshing separates the grain from seed.)
		Hamilton becomes enmeshed in an affair with Maria Reynolds and the subsequent extortion plot. The Hamiltons' fifth child, John Church, is born in the midst of the affair. In his professional life, Hamilton is the guiding force behind the creation of the Bank of the U.S.
1793	38 years old	**Louis XVI is guillotined in France during the French Revolution. The U.S. passes the first fugitive slave law requiring return of escaping slaves.**
		Robert Haeterick (or Heterick) receives the first U.S. patent for a stove made of cast iron. France introduces the first metric weight, the kilogram.
		Hamilton's critics accuse him of malfeasance through a series of resolutions proposed in Congress. He responds with a 20,000-word report and the resolutions do not pass. In August, a yellow fever epidemic breaks out in Philadelphia, where the Hamiltons live. Both Hamilton and his wife are stricken. They recover with the help of a childhood friend of Hamilton's, physician Edward Stevens.

Year	Hamilton's Age	Event
1794	39 years old	**Haiti, under the leadership of Toussaint L'Ouverture, revolts against France (during the French Revolution).**
		Sylvester Graham, the inventor of the graham cracker, is born.
		After a tax he proposed in 1791 to help pay federal debts led to widespread anger in Pennsylvania, Hamilton leads a military force to put down the protest. At roughly the same time, the Hamiltons' fifth child, 2-year-old John Church Hamilton, becomes gravely ill while Elizabeth is pregnant. He recovers but she miscarries.
1795	40 years old	**Fire destroys one-third of Copenhagen, Denmark, causing 18,000 casualties. The British capture Capetown, South Africa, from the Dutch and *La Marseillaise* becomes the French national anthem.**
		The British navy adopts limes (and lemons, which more expensive and difficult to obtain) as the standard food to be issued to sailors for prevention of scurvy. (Scurvy is a disease caused by lack of vitamin C, a nutrient found in citrus.) The term "limey" for a British sailor comes from this practice.
		Hamilton leaves his post as Secretary of the Treasury and moves back to New York from Philadelphia to resume private law practice.
1796	41 years old	**The first Independence Day celebration is held in the U.S. and the federal government issues the first U.S. passport.**
		American Cookery by Amelia Simmons, the first cookbook written by an American, is published in Hartford, Connecticut.
		Hamilton tries, but fails to get his preferred candidate (Charles Pinckney of South Carolina) elected President. Like Hamilton, the successful candidate, John Adams, is a Federalist, but the men had an active dislke for each other. Hamilton writes Washington's Farewell Address.

Year	Hamilton's Age	Event
1797	42 years old	**Albany replaces New York City as the capital of New York state.**
		H.L. Pernod becomes the first person to commercially manufacture absinthe.
		Angelica Church and her family move back to New York and live near the Hamiltons. The Hamiltons' sixth child, William Stephen, is born in August. The Reynolds affair again becomes fodder for the public humiliation of Hamilton and his family. In his own defense, Hamilton writes a 95-page booklet, with 37 pages of personal confession. Shortly after Hamilton's defense is published, his oldest child, Philip, becomes gravely ill with a high fever. Hamilton nurses him back to health.
1798–1799	43–44 years old	**New York state abolishes slavery and the metric system is established in France. George Washington dies in December 1799.**
		The term "cocktail" is first used, in a British newspaper, as part of a recipe for a drink served at a London pub.
		Washington again becomes army Commander-in-Chief, this time with Hamilton as second in command. As de facto army head, Hamilton counters the Fries Rebellion with overwhelming force; then President Adams pardons rebellion leaders. Hamilton collaborates with Aaron Burr on a project to create a private water company. However, the episode ends badly with a duel between Burr and Hamilton's brother-in-law, John Church. Neither man was hurt. Hamilton's father, James, dies on St. Vincent. Although they hadn't seen each other since James deserted the family, Hamilton sent his father regular support payments. Less than six months after his father's death, the Hamiltons' seventh child, Elizabeth, is born and a few weeks later, Washington dies.

Year	Hamilton's Age	Event
1800	45 years old	**Washington, D.C., becomes the U.S. Capitol and John Adams moves into the White House. Thomas Jefferson is elected as the third President of the U.S.**
		The first soup kitchens are opened in London.
		Hamilton drafts a bill to create a military academy, ends his own military service, and acts as co-counsel in a notable murder case with Burr. Increasingly disenchanted with Adams' presidency, he writes a 54-page critique that is not well received, even by his own allies. After 36 rounds of voting, Jefferson wins the presidency over Aaron Burr, largely due to Hamilton's intervention on Jefferson's behalf. Hamilton retreats from politics and begins building The Grange in northern Manhattan.
1801	46 years old	**Thomas Jefferson is the first U.S. President to be inaugurated in Washington, D.C.**
		Gail Borden, the inventor of the process of making condensed milk and the founder of the company that later become Borden Co., is born. Charles Cadbury, founder of the Cadbury Chocolate Company, is born.
		The Hamiltons' oldest child, Philip, dies in a duel at age 19, defending his father's honor. Hamilton is devastated and the death drives his oldest daughter, Angelica, insane.
1802	47 years old	**The French Revolution ends.**
		Osip Krichevsky, a Russian physician, invents the first modern production process for creating dried milk.
		The Hamiltons' eighth child, Philip (called "Little Phil"), is born.

Year	Hamilton's Age	Event
1803	48 years old	**The Louisiana Purchase is ratified by the U.S. Senate.**
		The apple parer is patented.
		Elizabeth's mother, Catharine Schuyler, dies.
1804	49 years old	**Napolen Bonaparte is proclaimed Emperor of France and Thomas Jefferson is re-elected as President of the U.S.**
		The Japanese company Mizkan is founded. Among the brands it later purchases are the American companies that make Ragu and Bertolli pasta sauces.
		Aaron Burr challenges Hamilton to a duel and shoots Hamilton, who dies the next day.

Chapter 2

Hamilton's World: 18TH Century West Indies and Colonial/ Early Federal America

The West Indies
of Hamilton's Youth

Looking out to the ocean from the West Indies islands where Hamilton grew up was a beautiful view. However, the islands themselves were not so hospitable for Hamilton or many of the other inhabitants.

Born on the island of Nevis into a family that was by no means rich, Hamilton moved to Christiansted, the capital of the Danish West Indies on the island of St. Croix, when he was ten years old. He lived on that 82-square mile island until he left for the American colonies in 1773 at the age of eighteen. Although Denmark owned and governed St. Croix at that time, its white population was a heterogeneous mix of European settlers, including French, British, Irish, and Scots as well as Danes.

Today, the island's economy depends on tourism, but in Hamilton's time, its fortunes were based on its major plantation crop, sugar, and sugar's byproducts rum and molasses. The plantations required slave labor and slaves far outnumbered the white inhabitants of St. Croix. By one count, at the end of the 1700s, the population of about 23,000 people consisted of 20,000 slaves (all African or of African descent), 1,000 "freed" persons of African descent, and 2,000 whites.[7]

Christiansted, a young city when Hamilton lived there, served as the port through which the products from the island's plantations were loaded on ships and sent to the American colonies and Europe. When Hamilton clerked at a trading house (basically an import-export business in today's terms), he could see how the bustling port operated and he spent time at the docks as well as in the company's nearby warehouse.

Rachel Hamilton's grocery store was located half a block from the city's Sunday Market. Slaves from the plantations could go to the market, sell their wares, and buy food and other necessities to take back to the plantation. Items sold at the market included hens, guinea fowl, ducks, pigs, goats, tubers, beans, cassava bread, and local varieties of fruits and vegetables such as mamee, papaya, guava, guavaberry, okra, bacuba, tannia, and bananas.[8] While it may seem odd that slaves could leave a plantation and be expected to return, keep in mind that St. Croix is a small island. It was tough to survive in the wild and not easy to disappear into the relatively small towns and capital city. Escaping off the island was also difficult.

There was also a slave market in Christiansted. Although the harshest conditions were undoubtedly on the plantations rather than in the city, Hamilton certainly saw slaves being bought and sold. He experienced slave ownership in his own family too. His mother owned two young slaves at the time of her death and willed them to Alexander and his brother James. The boys, however, did not inherit them, as the authorities ruled that their Lavien half-brother was entitled to claim their mother's entire estate.[9]

Colonial/Early Federal America from Hamilton's Perspective

Once he left St. Croix, Hamilton lived virtually all of his adult life in New York and Pennsylvania, with short stays in New Jersey when he first arrived in the colonies and during the Revolutionary War. His resided principally in New York City and in Philadelphia while that city functioned as the temporary capital of the United States during his time as Secretary of the Treasury. He also spent time at his in-laws' mansion in Albany, New York. To the extent that he traveled, it was mostly between those locations and in the course of the Revolutionary War, when he got as far south as Yorktown, Virginia.

In 1775, just a few years after Hamilton arrived from St. Croix, the population of the 13 colonies was about 2.5 million.[10] That is just about the current population of the city of Chicago. The population of New York state was about 200,000 and New York City had approximately 22,000 inhabitants. Albany, where Hamilton's in-laws, the Schuylers, lived, had 4,000 inhabitants, about 10 percent of whom were slaves. Chernow describes it as a "rough hewn" town, still heavily influenced by the Dutch language, traditions, and culture of its founders.[11]

By 1790, just after George Washington was elected the nation's first president and appointed Hamilton as the Secretary of the Treasury, the population of the United States had mushroomed. The country's total population was just under 4 million people[12] and New York state had over 340,000 inhabitants. At that time, there were just two cities with populations over 25,000: Philadelphia, with a population over 42,000, and New York City, with just over 33,000 inhabitants. Boston was a distant third with barely 18,000 inhabitants.[13] The fourth-largest city was Charleston, South Carolina. Less than 4 percent of the U.S. population lived in an urban area, defined as a town of at least 8,000 people. Compare those figures to the population in the 2010 national census. In 2010, the U.S. population was over 308 million, of whom 80 percent lived in an urban area.[14] The largest cities in 2010 were New York (over 8.1 million), Los Angeles (almost 3.8 million), and Chicago (almost 2.7 million). Boston was ranked 21st by population and Charleston, South Carolina, with fewer than 130,000 people, did not make it into the top 200 largest U.S. cities.[15]

New York City

New York City was much smaller geographically than it is today. The city began at the docks on the southern tip of Manhattan and basically ended just a bit farther north near Canal Street, in what is now known as Chinatown. It was a "winding maze of narrow streets, low buildings and bustling wharves."[16] The other boroughs and the rest of Manhattan were clusters of villages and farms in a rural setting. It was not until 1793 that the city fathers required buildings to be sequentially

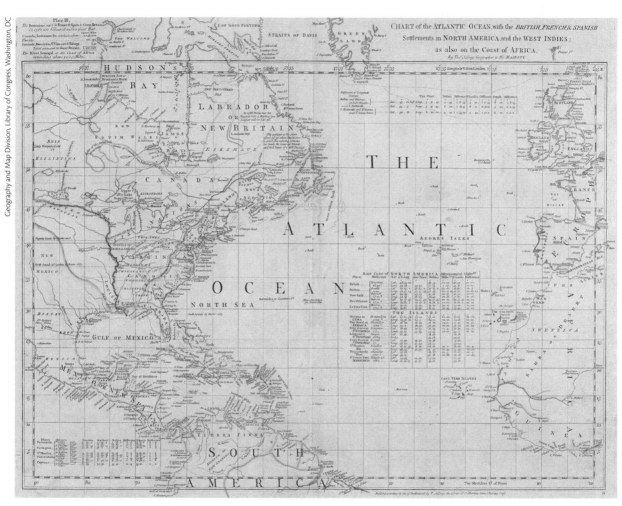

Chart of the Atlantic Ocean, with settlements in No. America, West Indies, and Cost of Africa. From *A General Topography of North America and the West Indies*. Plate III, Thomas Jeffrys, 1768. [sic]

numbered along a street; those numbered streets that now provide a grid pattern in Manhattan did not exist until almost a decade after Hamilton's death.[17] When Hamilton finished building The Grange, several miles north of Canal Street, that area was countryside where he could enjoy gardens and clean air.

Until 1762, New York had colonial America's second largest slave market, located at the foot of Wall Street.[18] While the proportion of slaves in New York City did not equal that in Southern cities, during colonial times as much as 20 percent of New York City's population were slaves and among its households, 41 percent had slaves. By contrast, the percentage of slave-holding households in Philadelphia was 6 percent and in Boston, 2 percent.[19]

New York was founded by the Dutch as a trading city and business was its lifeblood. Its cosmopolitan character and diverse population made New York City a welcoming environment for an enterprising and social young man like Hamilton. The theater scene had begun to flourish, and by the mid-1770s there were seven theaters in the city. Many found New York an exciting place filled with lovely river vistas and beautiful homes.

As to what New Yorkers appeared like to visitors, perhaps they were not so different then from the stereotype of a 21st-century New Yorker. When John Adams visited on his way to the Continental Congress in Philadelphia he made this observation:

"They talk very loud, very fast, and altogether. If they ask you a question, before you can utter three words of your answer, they will break out upon you again, and talk away."[20]

During the Revolutionary War, the British occupied the city. They arrived shortly after the signing of the Declaration of Independence on July 4, 1776, and the last British troops did not leave until late 1783.[21] Hamilton was part of the colonial army that retreated from New York City. During the War, the British used the city as a detention center for captured Patriots, detaining them on ships and in a variety of public and private buildings. The British even kept some of their prisoners in churches and the classrooms of King's College, where Hamilton had been studying until the war broke out. Altogether the British detained about 30,000 prisoners in New York City at one point or another during the Revolutionary War, close to the entire civilian population at that time. The day the last British soldier left New York, November 25, 1783, became a holiday called Evacuation Day. Although no longer celebrated, it was a popular holiday in New York for more than a century after the end of the Revolutionary War.[22] Because Hamilton was both a New Yorker and a veteran with first-hand knowledge of the occupation and its devastation, it is likely that the holiday was meaningful for him. History records that he attended a special dinner to mark the occasion at least once.

Chapter 3

Cooking In Hamilton's Time

The Kitchen, Cooking Equipment, and Furniture

Kitchens were neither comfortable nor easy places in which to cook during Hamilton's time. At The Grange, built in 1802, the kitchen was in the basement.[23] In large homes built in the decades before, such as the home Elizabeth Schuyler grew up in near Albany, New York, kitchens were typically "out buildings," located on the property but far enough away to keep the smells and hustle and bustle away from the main house.[24] The practice of putting kitchens in outbuildings prevailed even in cities such as Philadelphia, if the home and its grounds were large enough to accommodate separate structures.[25] With no air conditioning and with a constant fire to cook food, the kitchen could be both hot and buggy in the summer. Without modern ventilation, the area near the hearth would be warm or even hot in the winter, but the rest of the room was likely to be drafty and cold.

Most cooking took place in or over the open hearth (the floor) of a fireplace. Hearths were dangerous, often smoky, and generally inefficient. However, a skilled and experienced cook could use the hearth to cook using a variety of methods:

- Frying (using flame heat underneath with a pan between the flame and the item being cooked; frying requires using fat, i.e. butter, oil, or lard)
- Stewing (cooking meat, poultry and/or vegetables in liquid and serving them in the gravy that results from the cooking)
- Poaching (submerging meat, poultry, or fish in barely simmering liquid)
- Boiling (cooking in liquid that is brought to, and kept at, its boiling point)
- Broiling (cooking using direct flame on top) or grilling (cooking using direct flame from below)
- Roasting (cooking with radiant or indirect heat)
- Baking[26]

Baking was done in the hearth with a Dutch oven, which is a deep, heavy pot with a lid in which a cook placed dough. Those who could afford it had a beehive-shaped brick oven built into the fireplace or placed outside. Such ovens were similar to those now used in brick oven pizza restaurants. If a family could not afford an oven, in many areas a cook could bring dough to a local baker who would rent space in his large oven.

The hearth had to be wide and deep enough to accommodate several different types of cooking at once. In some cases, the fireplace might be eight or ten feet wide.[27] In most places in the American colonies and later the states, wood was plentiful so it was a major source of the fuel needed to keep a fire going for cooking. In order to keep the wood off a hearth floor to let air circulate, a hearth would be equipped with andirons, also called firedogs.

It took skill, experience, and strength to keep the fire (or more precisely, several small fires in the same hearth) at the proper level of heat for each type of cooking and to move and remove heavy pots and pans. Those who tended the fire used tongs to move burning wood and peels (long-handled shovels with flat surfaces) to move hot coals or charcoal. They removed embers from the fire using a fire pan.

It was common to keep the fires going all day, then bury them in ash during the night so they would not die out, reviving them in the morning. In order to change a food's cooking temperature, a cook would either move the food closer to, or farther from, the fire or change the intensity of the fire. Either way, it was an imprecise way to cook.

For those who were able to afford them (especially in urban areas), stew stoves, also known as potagers, became more common during Hamilton's lifetime. Built like benches, stew stoves had openings fitted with an iron grate. Below the grate, a firebox held a small fire burning coal or charcoal.

Just before the end of the eighteenth century (1796), a loyalist named Benjamin Thompson designed a shallower fireplace that burned less wood but gave off more heat due to its redesigned chimney. It was called a Rumford fireplace, after the birthplace of Thompson's wife. Although the new design was not limited to kitchens (Jefferson

Hearth with cooking utensils

installed eight Rumford fireplaces throughout Monticello in renovations he began in 1796)[28], for this book's purposes the main benefit of the Rumford fireplace was that it was an advancement in how kitchen hearths were built and operated. When building his new home, The Grange, Hamilton included a Rumford-type fireplace in the kitchen.[29]

In order to accommodate all of the necessary pots, pans, and kettles, hearths had long iron bars up one side and over the top. In the early part of the 18th century, pots hung over the hearth on a pole with an extension and a hook called a trammel. By the time Hamilton was born, the poles had evolved into cranes that could swing into the front or back of the hearth, so the cook did not have to step far into the hearth to get to the pot. The trammel (with chains) could raise and lower pots and kettles, and move them from the back to the front of the hearth.[30]

Pots had bulging sides and a cover while kettles had sloped sides with no cover. The largest kettles, called cauldrons, could be so valuable that they would be passed down in wills when the owner of the house died.

For those dishes that needed to be even closer to the fire, cooks used 3-legged pans. Small ones with rounded bottoms were called posnets or pipkins, while the larger versions with flat bottoms were called spiders or spyders.[31]

Roasting could be done one of four ways:

- with a spit that sat between low andirons with a pan for the drippings
- by a spit set inside a tin or copper drum cut in half
- by a cord suspended from a hook on the hearth
- in a reflector oven or tin kitchen, a tin or copper drum cut in half with a spit inside

As mentioned, major baking was generally done once a week in Dutch ovens in a beehive oven, or at a nearby baker's oven.

Making toast required holding the bread close to the fire for a short time. A common piece of equipment for toasting was a wrought iron contraption mounted on feet with a set of swiveling "claws" that held slices of bread.

Cooking utensils used to stir, ladle, or flip food cooking on the hearth had to be long-handled so that they could be used to reach the food no matter where it was located in the hearth.

Furniture in a kitchen tended to do double duty. For example, a chest used for storage would also be used on top as a work surface. The same was true for a hutch. To save space and also for decoration, it was common to hang items that could include brass and copper utensils and plates. Dr. Alexander Hamilton (no relation), a Scottish-born physician and traveler throughout the mid-Atlantic colonies in the mid-1700s, wrote about the Dutch kitchens he saw near Albany, the area where Hamilton's in-laws, the Schuylers, lived. Dr. Hamilton noted the cleanliness of the kitchens and that "they hang earthen or delft plates and dishes all-round the walls in manner of picture, having a hole drilled thro (sic) the edge of the plate or dish and a loop of ribbon put into it to hang it by."[32]

Of course, without electricity, a kitchen in a basement or after the sun went down would be a dreary place in which to prepare food. Candles may be romantic, but they are not ideal for providing good light for cooking or baking. Bill Bryson notes in his book *At Home: A Short History of Private Life,* "[A] good candle provides barely a hundredth of the illumination of a single 100-watt light bulb. Open your refrigerator door and you summon forth more light than the total amount enjoyed by most households in the 18th century."[33]

Food Storage

In Hamilton's time, if one did not have access to ice from a frozen pond, lake, or river, and space enough to store it, the options for cool storage were limited. Thomas Jefferson had a separate ice house at Monticello, where he stored chunks of the frozen Rivanna River from winter through to the following October, enabling his household staff to preserve meat and butter and even to make ice cream.[34] That was not an option for the Hamiltons who lived in crowded lower Manhattan and in urban Philadelphia. While the Hamiltons may have had ice delivered for special occasions or special items, they probably bought food more frequently, stored most fresh food only for short periods, and relied on a variety of techniques to preserve foods.

Modern cooks can buy food in bulk, on their own schedule, and refrigerate or freeze it until it's used days, weeks, or even months later. In Hamilton's day, city dwellers shopped daily or close to it. And the food they purchased had to come from close by, as there were no refrigerated trucks to transport perishable foods long distances. The typical contemporary description of how long meat, a staple of the diet in Hamilton's time, lasted is that it had to be eaten or preserved within twenty-four hours of the animal being butchered.

The two types of common storage were cool storage for fruits, vegetables, and even eggs, and dry storage for grains and other items. Cool storage, sometimes called a "root cellar," might be below-ground and would be dark and cool enough to store onions, potatoes, turnips, and other root vegetables, as well as fruits such as apples. The dry storage location would keep flours, beans, and similar items from rotting.

In Hamilton's time, cooks used a number of techniques besides cool storage to preserve foods without refrigeration. They "potted" meat, mixing it with other ingredients and storing it in earthen jars. The resulting mincemeat was often used in pies. Meats could also be dried, salted (using a light coating of salt to preserve meat was called "corning" as in corned beef), or smoked. Vegetables were typically preserved by pickling them in a vinegar-based liquid, but cucumbers and cabbage could also be preserved through fermentation, making them into sour pickles and sauerkraut. Beans and grains were dried. Fruits were dried, or preserved in sugar syrup (jams or jellies), or preserved in alcohol, such as cherries in brandy.

Who Cooked?

In homes of the well-to-do, a still-familiar situation generally prevailed: men did not cook and had little to do with the housekeeping chores relating to cooking and food. The "lady of the house" would supervise, which meant that she had to know how to do the various activities involved in preparing food, serving, entertaining, and maintaining a kitchen. However, women such as Elizabeth Hamilton had servants or slaves who did the actual cooking, serving, cleaning, and related tasks.

It took more than one person to do all of the cooking for a large family such as the Hamiltons, especially because Alexander and Elizabeth liked to entertain. Everything had to be made by hand, and tasks related to marketing and preparing the food had to be done almost daily. Imagine preparing large multicourse dinners without a refrigerator, freezer, mixer, or food processor. Then imagine cooking all the dishes for daily meals on an open hearth, rather than on easily controlled stovetop burners and in an oven with temperature settings.

For formal dinner parties with numerous guests, the hosts had to have butlers and maids to serve the food and remove and wash the numerous dishes. Although the Hamiltons did not have household slaves late in their life together (Angelica Church even wrote to her sister in 1804 bemoaning the fact that Elizabeth did not have slaves to help her prepare for a large party the Hamiltons planned to give), they may have had household slaves earlier in their marriage and certainly had servants during their entire marriage.

The number of people who cooked and served meals was dependent, of course, on the employing family's means and the size of the group that needed to be fed. When both the Washingtons and the Hamiltons lived in Philadelphia, George and Martha Washington had numerous domestic servants for their household entourage, which included extended family and friends.[35] Their housekeeper and a steward oversaw others, including a cook, maids, and a butler, as well as others who could help in the kitchen and serving chores on an "as needed" basis.[36] Another large and wealthy Philadelphia family of the period, the Chews (who were friends of the Washingtons and others in the Hamiltons' social circle), typically had a regular staff of around seventeen, including "free" servants, indentured servants, and slaves, plus two washerwomen, a seamstress, and others hired on an occasional basis. The cook had help from nine people on the regular staff, five women and four men (a combination of slaves and white servants) who performed kitchen and serving chores as well as other duties.[37] While the Hamilton household was reasonably large, they were not as wealthy as many of those with whom they socialized. Still, they certainly had at least a few servants who would have cooked and served their food.

Cooks who were "free" servants (not indentured servants or slaves) were typically paid about $40 to $55 a year in the late eighteenth century in Philadelphia, and more if they could create fancy confections; less skilled kitchen workers and maids earned half that. By the end of the eighteenth century, domestic servants in New York earned about $8 a month, or $96 a year.[38] Cooks and those who helped them (along with other domestic servants) typically began work by candlelight in the early morning, perhaps as early as 5 a.m. They would work until late in the evening, after supper had been served, everything cleaned up, and preparations made for the next day's meals.[39]

Risks in the Kitchen

In the eighteenth century, there was no system to track workplace injuries and none of the resources we have available today to understand the relative risks of various activities. While we may not be able to determine whether there were more cooking injuries in Hamilton's time or whether they were more severe than they are today, we can imagine how cooking injuries might have occurred. Working with an open fire certainly carries risk and a cook or maid had to be careful to keep her long skirts away from the embers and flames when moving pots and pans around the hearth. Also, pots and pans were made of heavy cast iron and similar materials and tended to be large to accommodate portions for big families and gatherings. One can imagine the strained backs and scalding injuries that must have occurred from moving those heavy pieces around.

Ingredients and Popular Dishes

Without refrigeration and easy methods to transport fresh food ingredients, even wealthy people ate what was locally available. The "buy local" movement was not a matter of choice; it was a necessity in Hamilton's time. Fresh fish are highly perishable, so those preparing fish dishes in Hamilton's time had to use whatever was most plentiful in nearby waters. A New Englander might use cod, common in the Atlantic waters off those northern states,[40] while a Mid-Atlantic cook might utilize flounder,[41] and a Southerner might gravitate to a recipe for catfish.[42] Those who lived inland (e.g., Albany, where Hamilton's in-laws lived and where he spent a good deal of time) would have used fish caught in nearby lakes and rivers, rather than saltwater fish from the ocean far away from their home.

Several ingredients that we consider luxuries today were more plentiful and less expensive in Hamilton's time. For example, lobsters were abundant and sometimes grew to be five to six feet in the waters around New York in that time period. Oysters were so plentiful that they were commonly sold as street food. Some of those not sold locally were pickled and sent to the West Indies. Like lobsters, oysters grew large in that era. One person described a single oyster as enough for several mouthfuls. "Oyster cellars" or saloons sold "all you can eat" oysters for six cents. "Although it was said that if a patron ate too many, the waiter would slip him a bad one."[43]

Certain items were used as ingredients that we do not use today in American cuisine. Most of the ones that would strike a modern person as most bizarre involve animals and animal parts. Popular recipes of the time featured turtles (roasted or in soup), eel, pigeons, calves' heads, and beef tongue. We cannot imagine making a blood pudding with half a pint of lamb, pig, or goose blood or a minced pie made with the feet or tongues of beef cattle.

Even some ingredients that we still use frequently today vary from the versions common during Hamilton's time. Their meat was tougher and their butter tended to be saltier than ours. Their sugar was hard, sold in loaves or cones from which a cook had to pound or chip off the amount required. Eggs were smaller in Hamilton's time and, of course, they were not graded for size. That meant recipes specified more eggs than we would typically use today (most American recipes call for "large" eggs) and that the number of eggs was less precise than it would be in a modern recipe that uses uniformly sized eggs. Flour used in Hamilton's time was heavier than ours, so following a recipe for baked goods from that time means using more flour to get the same result.[44] Raisins were larger in those days and they contained seeds. Recipes that called for them often instructed the cook to remove the seeds or "stone" and to chop the fruit.[45]

While the term ketchup (catsup or catchup) was used in Hamilton's time, it didn't refer to the slightly spicy-sweet tomato condiment that we call by that name today. Instead, it was a term for a method of creating a vinegar-based condiment from various ingredients such as walnuts and mushrooms. In her eighteenth century classic book, *The Experienced English Housekeeper*, Elizabeth Raffald provides a recipe for "a Catchup to keep Seven Years." The ingredients include "two quarts of the oldest strong beer you can get," a quart of red wine, three quarters of a pound of anchovies, shallots, and spices.[46]

Ingredients and foods still common today were not always used or treated in the same way. Spices were often used in greater quantities in Hamilton's time than we would use them. Their aromas could hide a disagreeable odor if food was going bad, and once people got used to the heavy concentrations of spices, that became the norm. Today, with better food storage methods, we do not eat food that is "off" and so do not use spices for that purpose. Also, we tend to use spices with a lighter touch to enhance rather than hide flavors. During Hamilton's time, salt was a common preservative, so cooks and diners would sprinkle vinegar on foods to counteract any lingering salty taste.[47] Today, we rarely use salt as a preservative and we are conscious of the need to lower our sodium consumption. Therefore, if we use vinegar as a condiment, it is typically for its own taste. Beer or ale was a popular drink in Hamilton's day and remains so today. But in that period, beer was a common breakfast drink, while today we save it for later in the day or evening.

Finally, there are foods we eat today that people in Hamilton's time avoided. They believed that tomatoes and potatoes were poisonous. In the case of potatoes, the belief had no basis in fact. The tomato situation was more complicated; there were poisonings of wealthy people who ate tomatoes. However, the poisonings did not occur because of any inherent problem with the tomatoes. Instead, the problem occurred because the wealthy diners tended to use pewter plates containing lead. The acid in the tomatoes caused the lead to leach out of the plates, resulting in lead poisoning in some cases. Needless to say, both potatoes and tomatoes are now well accepted as components of the modern American diet. Another food scorned in Hamilton's time was peanuts. A common snack food now, peanuts were considered food for the poor and for animals in that period, not for people who had other options.[48]

Chapter 4

Dining with Alexander Hamilton

Eating in the West Indies

We can't know for sure what Hamilton ate growing up in the West Indies, but we do know that, as a white person, he lived a relatively poor existence until he moved into the Stevens's home. That probably meant a diet heavy in bread and dried fish. The main crops of the islands, sugar, molasses, and rum, would have been available and his mother did run a grocery for a time. Maybe he ate traditional West Indian foods such as kallalo (a vegetable stew made with a green leafy plant such as amaranth or taro and sometimes with a bit of inexpensive meat such as a salted pigtail), fungi (a cornmeal dish), saltfish, lobster, red beans and rice, plantains, curried chicken, stewed mutton, conch fritters, and Johnny cakes.

Spicy foods containing local chili peppers were popular. Perhaps the most popular pepper grown in the West Indies, the Scotch bonnet, comes in hot and hotter varieties. The latter can be more than 50 to 100 times spicier than a jalapeño pepper. If Hamilton liked hot peppers, he might have carried that taste into adulthood and enjoyed a specialty both of the West Indies and Philadelphia called Pepper Pot Soup (see the recipe on page 75).

The prosperous Stevens family presumably ate well. Like Hamilton, the Stevens family was of Scottish ancestry. One visitor to the islands described such a family eating a typical Scottish breakfast of the time, which might have included a varied array of porridges or other hot cereals, meats, cheeses, eggs, fish, breads, coffee, tea, and even rum.[49] Following the European custom in that time, the Stevens family probably ate their large meal at midday, including several kinds of meats, fish, and poultry, along with numerous other dishes. A smaller meal, called supper, would have been typical in the evening. Of course, on St. Croix wealthy islanders like the Stevens family would have had access to local fruits that would not have made their way (by ship, without refrigeration) to the American colonies or Europe. And although neither Hamilton nor the Stevens family were of Danish descent, St. Croix was a Danish possession in the mid-1700s, so they might have eaten Red Grout, a compote made of guava or other local fruits thickened with tapioca. Red Grout is the St. Croix version of the Danish dessert, rødgrød.[50]

Eating on the Mainland

During Hamilton's time, the average American's diet was meat-centered and heavy on bread and other starches. They tended to eat vegetables only in small amounts, often cooked in fat or covered in sauce. Colonists and Americans during the early Federal period did not drink much water or milk because those drinks tended to carry disease. Instead, they drank chocolate, tea, and coffee made with water from outside the city where it was cleaner, and alcoholic beverages. (During periods when tea was taxed by the British or being boycotted by the colonists, they avoided that beverage.) Hard cider, wines, and fortified wines such as sherry and Madeira were favorites, along with rum from the West Indies and later whiskey.

As an adult, Hamilton would not have had easy access to the local fruits common in the West Indies, but he still could have obtained rum, molasses, sugar, lemons, nutmeg, and allspice imported from the islands.

Rum was the most popular drink in the eighteenth century. Wines and fortified wines such as sherry and Madeira, imported from the Azores, were also popular.[51] Hamilton definitely enjoyed wine. He drank wines paired with each course during fancy dinners, such as the one Jefferson hosted (see pages 49–50), and in the weeks before his death in 1804, his papers indicate that he bought $150 worth of wine.[52]

Wheat was the most popular grain in the Mid-Atlantic, used for baking breads and sweets. Elizabeth Schuyler grew up in a household heavily influenced by her family's Dutch traditions. Crisp spiced cookies called speculaas or speculoos, doughnuts, and butter cake or boterkoek would have been common sweets in her home, especially during the holidays.[53]

In Hamilton's time, meat, especially beef, was a staple. Mutton, pork, veal, and animal parts rarely eaten today, such as tripe, were also popular. We know that the Hamiltons ate those because they are on a list of the Hamilton family expenses from 1791.[54]

Dining with the Family

Before discussing the food, it is worth noting that dining rooms are a relatively new feature of houses. When Hamilton's in-laws, the Schuylers, moved into their home in 1765, there was no such thing as a dining room. Dining chambers became popular in the U.S. only after the Revolutionary War. Before that time, the Schuylers and families such as theirs dined in any available spaces. For the Schuylers, that was in the central hallway in summer and in one of the parlors during other months.[55] Once Alexander and Elizabeth married, they presumably would have taken to the then-new custom of creating a special space for dining. And when Hamilton designed The Grange just after 1800, it did contain a dining room.[56]

Breakfast in Hamilton's world was typically not elaborate; it was often leftovers from the previous day's larger meals. Those of Dutch ancestry, such as Elizabeth and her family, frequently ate bread and butter for breakfast with slices of dried beef[57] or bread and butter with cheese and milk.[58] Some, especially among the Dutch, also liked hot cereal, one type being a cornmeal and milk porridge called "suppawn." Shoofly (or shoo-fly) pie, made with molasses from the West Indies, was popular in Pennsylvania, where Hamilton spent much time. A dry version of the pie, like a coffee cake inside a pie crust, was a common breakfast food in that region.[59] Hamilton would have been familiar with molasses from his childhood in the West Indies, so it makes sense that he would have known of, and perhaps enjoyed, the shoo-fly pie "coffee cake."

While the most popular beverages for breakfast were beer and hard cider, there is at least some evidence suggesting that Hamilton may have preferred coffee.[60] Tea and hot chocolate were also popular. Of course, the drink an individual chose depended on availability and personal preference.[61]

Although the Hamiltons had access to fresh milk when they stayed with Elizabeth's family in Albany, that was not the case when they lived in lower Manhattan or Philadelphia. Because milk spoils quickly without refrigeration, those who lived far from dairies and did not own a cow typically did not drink milk or give it to children. Cheese, which is easier to safely store, was more readily available.

The Hamilton's third son, James, reminisced about breakfast with his family, describing his mother seated, as was her wont, at the head of the table with a napkin in her lap, cutting slices of bread and spreading them with butter for the younger boys, who standing at her side, read in turn a chapter in the Bible or a portion of Goldsmith's Rome. When the lessons were finished, the father and the elder children were called to breakfast, after which the boys were packed off to school.[62]

A British traveler described breakfast with George and Martha Washington in Philadelphia as follows: "Mrs. Washington herself made tea and coffee for us. On the table were two small plates of sliced tongue, dry toast, bread and butter, etc., but no broiled fish as is the general custom."[63] This description could have applied to Hamilton's breakfast as well.

The largest meal of the day was the dinner meal at midday, at least until the end of the 1700s. It might have had a number of courses, including soup, several types of meats, fish, stews, and sweets. The meal at the end of the day, supper, was typically lighter and with fewer courses than dinner. Toward the end of the 1700s, those following the English style moved the dinner meal to the late afternoon.[64]

With many children to feed and sometimes-strained finances, the Hamiltons' large midday meals at home may not have been elegant affairs, but they likely would have included ample food. Along with the several meats customarily served, they enjoyed potatoes and turnips (root vegetables that can stay fresh in root cellars or other cool storage for considerable periods), as well as apples and pears. While entertaining would have likely involved a number of courses and different dishes, when they ate as a family, the Hamiltons might well have enjoyed a large, one-pot meal such as a stew with vegetables.

Supper would have been a meal of leftovers, porridge, or similar foods. This light meal could be similar to breakfast or more of what we might eat for lunch today.

No Take-Out or Restaurant Meals for the Hamilton Family

Family dining was an at-home activity in Hamilton's time. There were no freestanding restaurants, and typically, families did not go out to eat in the establishments that existed for dining away from home. Eating out was usually the preserve of men with business affairs to conduct, whether at a coffeehouse, an oyster cellar, a tavern, or a dining room in a hotel.[65] Hamilton certainly visited at least one famous tavern, Fraunces, which opened in 1762 and operates today in renovated space at the same location where it existed in Hamilton's day, near his home in lower Manhattan. Another dining-out locale not too far from his home was City Hotel on Broadway. It opened in 1794 and served "family-style" meals (but, ironically, not to families) at long tables.[66]

Hamilton as a Dinner Guest

Elaborate dinners were part of the social scene that Hamilton enjoyed so much. Those meals could last for hours and included many dishes, prepared and served by slaves, indentured, or "free" servants.

The Hamiltons dined with the George and Martha Washington at numerous points during their decades-long relationship. They also socialized with numerous other luminaries of their time, such as John Jay, James Madison (with whom Hamilton was friendly at the time they wrote *The Federalist Papers*, even though they later became estranged), local political figures, and society figures such as William and Ann Willing Bingham in Philadelphia. Such dinners would have been opulent affairs, including many more courses and a greater variety of dishes than one would normally find at a 21st-century dinner party.

One example was the dinner that George Washington hosted at the Morris-Jumel Mansion in New York on July 10, 1790, for members of his new administration. The eighteen guests included the Secretaries of Treasury (Hamilton), War (Henry Knox), State (Thomas Jefferson), and Vice-President John Adams, along with their wives. The party spent a full day touring the ruins of a Revolutionary War battlefield later called Fort Washington, and then went to the house that had been Washington's military headquarters.[67] A cook hired by Washington prepared a large dinner for the guests, which they ate outside because there was no room large enough to seat them all for a meal.[68]

Men also dined socially without their wives. An example of Washington's hospitality "for men only" was a dinner Hamilton attended in Philadelphia on February 20, 1792, a few days before Washington's sixtieth birthday. The guests were Alexander Hamilton, John Adams, Henry Knox, Thomas Jefferson, and President Washington's private secretary, Tobias Lear. The dinner included "soups, broiled pork, goose, roast beef, mutton chops, hominy, cabbage potatoes, fried tripe, onions, fish, mince pies, torts, cheese and a variety of vegetables." The President and his guests washed down their food with beer and cider. Dessert was "chocolate pudding, cream trifle, macarons, and apple pie." After dinner they sampled several wines, including nonsparkling or still champagne. Jefferson explained to the assembled group that the still variety was considered in France to be preferable to the more common sparkling champagne. According to the diary of William Maclay, this was typical of the dinners served by President Washington.[69]

Another dinner Washington served had a similarly large menu. One guest, Joshua Brooks, remembered:

> ...leg of boiled pork at the head of the table, a goose at the foot and in between roast beef, round cold boiled beef, mutton chops, hominy, cabbage, potatoes, pickles, fried tripe and onions. Beverages offered during dinner, wine, porter and beer. The table cloth was wiped off before the second course of mince pies, tarts, cheese. The cloth was removed and port and Madeira served along with nuts, raisins, apples.[70]

Jefferson Hosted Hamilton at a Meal that Changed History

Certainly, the most famous dinner that Hamilton attended was the one that Thomas Jefferson hosted on June 20, 1790. He invited only two guests: Hamilton and James Madison.

At that dinner, the three men forged a compromise. In exchange for Hamilton's support for locating the nation's capital in the South on the Potomac River (now Washington, D.C.), Madison would rally Virginia's support for Hamilton's plan to have the federal government assume state debts as part of his vision to establish a strong federal monetary policy.

James Hemings, Jefferson's slave (and Sally Hemings's brother), a French-trained chef, prepared the dinner. It began with salad served with wine jelly made from boiled calves feet (hooves), Madeira wine, milk, lemon juice, and sugar. Then there were two first, or main, courses. The first was capon (a rooster that is castrated to improve the quality of its meat), which was stuffed with Virginia ham and chestnut purée, artichoke bottoms, and truffles, with a bit of cream, white wine, and chicken stock. A sauce made with Calvados, an apple brandy from the French region of Normandy, was served

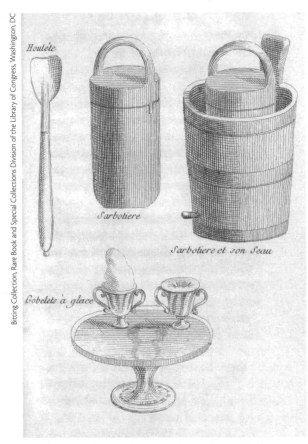

Houlete

Sarbotiere

Sarbotiere et son Seau

Gobelets à glace

Ice cream-making implements and serving utensils from *L'art de bien faire les glaces*

in Tuscany. The second part of the first, or main, course was an Americanized version of the famed French dish *boeuf a la mode*. That meat dish was served with another red wine, but this time from the Burgundy region of France. Before dessert there was a sweets course that included meringues, macaroons, and a deep-fried egg-and-flour cookie known as a "bell fritter." Dessert was vanilla ice cream enclosed in a warm pastry, which was described as like a cream puff. There is some dispute over exactly what this dessert was—how the pastry worked and whether it was like a modern profiterole split open or closer to ice cream enclosed in a puff pastry crust. However it looked, apparently Hamilton was enthralled. One author of an account of this dinner described his reaction as "Hamilton positively exulted as if his Assumption Bill had just passed by a huge vote."[71]

A Hamilton Dinner Party

When Alexander and Elizabeth Hamilton gave a dinner party, who would have attended, what would it have been like, and what would they have served?

The guest list, of course, would have depended on who was living close by at the time. Hamilton did give work-related dinners, such as the one he hosted for Jefferson when the latter returned from France, and a dinner for military officers who served with him.[72]

alongside the capon. Jefferson, who was quite a wine connoisseur, had brought back numerous wines from Europe and he enjoyed choosing the proper wine to go with each course. He served this course with a red wine from Montepulciano,

But if we look simply at who they would have wanted to entertain, several close friends of Hamilton's come immediately to mind:

- Robert Troup, who lived with the Hamiltons at the Schuyler's home in Albany for a time.
- Edward Stevens, his physician and close friend from St. Croix who saved Alexander and Elizabeth when they contracted yellow fever.
- Hercules Mulligan, one of the first people Hamilton met when he arrived in New York as an eighteen-year-old.
- John Jay, a Founding Father, friend, and a co-author of *The Federalist Papers.*
- Nicholas Fish, with whom Hamilton served in the military during the Revolutionary War.
- William Livingston, a Founding Father who helped Hamilton when he first came to the colonies.
- Rufus King, another Founding Father who worked with Hamilton, Gouverneur Morris, Madison, and William Samuel Johnson to prepare the final draft of the United States Constitution.
- Gouverneur Morris, a Founding Father who was also on the drafting committee for the Constitution, and a close friend. (He gave the eulogy at Hamilton's funeral in 1804.)

And, of course, both of the Hamiltons would have wanted as guests Elizabeth's sister Angelica and her husband (their brother-in-law), John Church.

The meal would have been eaten on their gold-embossed tableware, a gift from the Churches. Conversation would have been lively, as Hamilton was known to be an excellent dinner companion. And there would have been lots of wine, which Hamilton liked to drink on social occasions at home as well as elsewhere.

The Menu for a Hamilton Dinner Party

As to the menu, there would probably have been soup, followed by many meat and vegetable dishes, with a number of fruits, nuts, and sweets afterwards. The custom at that time was to serve all of the dishes for a course at once and each course had several pieces of tableware, so the table would have been laden with serving tureens and plates.

In a popular cookbook of the period, *The Art of Cookery Made Plain and Easy,*[73] Hannah Glasse lays out menus for a party in each month of the year. Glasse provides three courses, consisting of about eight to ten different dishes. Needless to say, the Hamiltons might have opted for a less elaborate meal, but even at half the number of dishes, it is still quite a feast.

THE ORDER OF A
MODERN BILL OF FARE,

FOR EACH MONTH,

In the Manner the Dishes are to be placed upon the Table.

FOR
JANUARY.

FIRST COURSE.

Soup.

Leg of Lamb.   Petit Patties.   Boiled Chickens.

Chicken and Veal Pie.   Cod's Head.   Roasted Beef.

Tongue.   Patties.   Scotch Collops.

Vermicelli Soup.

SECOND COURSE.

Roasted Turkey.

Marinated Smelts.   Tartles.   Mince Pies.

Roast Sweetbreads.   Stands of Jellies.   Larks.

Almond Tort.   Maids of Honour.   Lobsters.

Woodcocks.

THIRD COURSE.

Morels.

Artichoke Bottoms.   Dutch Beef scraped.   Macaroni.

Custards.   Cut Pastry.   Black Caps.

Scolloped Oysters.   Potted Chars.   Stewed Celery.

Rabbit Fricaseed.

N. B. In your first course always observe to send up all Kinds of Garden Stuff suitable to your Meat, &c. in different dishes, on a Water-dish filled with hot Water on the side Table ; and all your Sauce in Boats or Basons, to answer one another at the corners.

January Bill of Fare from *The Art of Cookery Made Plain and Easy*

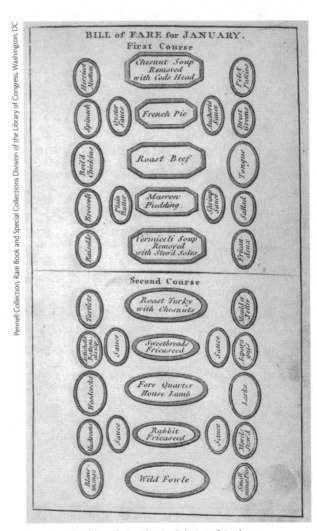

January Bill of Fare from *The English Art of Cookery*

Another cookbook of the era, *The English Art of Cookery, According to the Present Practice* by Richard Briggs,[74] provides menus that are even more elaborate. Those menus, in diagram form for each month, show where each dish should be laid on the table. Briggs prescribes two courses for a "bill of fare." Each of those courses included five main dishes set down the center of the table, with five dishes on each long side of the table, and two sauces or condiments on each side, set between the lines of main dishes and side dishes. Not counting the sauces and condiments, those dinners included fifteen dishes in each course for a total of thirty dishes in a dinner, not including the fruits, nuts, and sweets served afterwards in this number.

Even setting the table for dessert or tea could involve rather intricate details. In his book *The Complete Confectioner*, Frederic Nutt set out a variety of such tables for sweets. Opposite is one that Nutt suggests.

At their dinner party, the Hamiltons might have served:

First Course (with appropriate sauces and "garden stuff," as Hannah Glasse termed it)

- Green Pea Soup
- Roasted Beef
- Lamb Pie
- Turbot

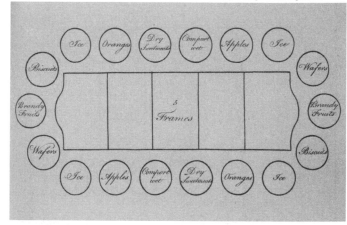

Diagram of table of sweets from *The Complete Confectioner*

Second Course (with appropriate sauces)

- Scolloped Oysters
- Roasted Sweetbreads
- Fricasee of Rabbits
- Small Roasted Turkey
- Peas
- Stewed Celery

Third Course (with appropriate sauces)

- Matelot of Eels
- Preserved Oranges
- Green Gooseberry Tart
- Mushrooms
- Raisins
- Lambs Tails *a la Braise*

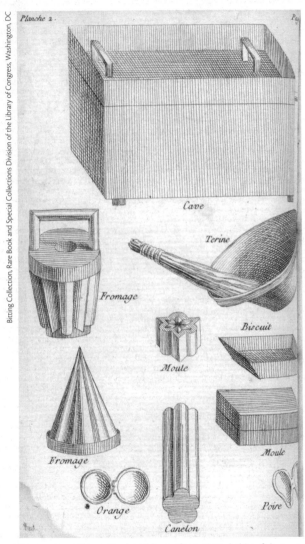

Ice cream molds and related items from *L'art de bien faire les glaces*

One item we can be fairly sure they would have included after such a meal is ice cream. Known in the English-speaking world since the mid-1700s, ice cream was advertised in New York City as early as 1777.[75] At that time, ice cream was typically made in America and England using fruit or other flavoring and cream, cooled in a tub of ice and salt, and stirred while it thickened. It was often served in a mold or pastry shells.

Travelers such as Jefferson and Angelica Church expanded Americans' ice cream horizons by introducing them to the French, custard-style ice cream. We know that the Hamiltons loved ice cream and they supposedly introduced George and Martha Washington to the joys of ice cream when the Hamiltons hosted the Washingtons at a dinner in 1789.[76] Hamilton himself enjoyed it at the June 1790 dinner at Jefferson's home. So even though we might not be familiar with many of the items served earlier in the meal, we can be sure that by dessert, a twenty-first century American would feel right at home eating a Hamilton dinner.

Chapter 5

Explanation of Recipes

Each recipe is presented in two forms: the original recipe from the Hamilton-era cookbook where I found it and my adaptation of the recipe, using twenty-first century ingredients, measurements, and techniques.

But first, a few notes…

Why does this book cite various editions of the same cookbook?

Old cookbooks were often published in different editions, sometimes decades apart. The recipes and book format often changed substantially from one edition to the next. I reviewed multiple editions of several of the old cookbooks cited; sometimes the recipe or menu I decided to adapt was in multiple versions of the book and at other times it appeared only in one version.

How close are the adaptations to the original recipes?

I tried to preserve the basic intent of the original recipes, while making them accessible to the modern cook/reader.

In some cases, an ingredient was not widely available, so I used the closest substitute. For example, in Hamilton's time, many recipes, both for sweet and savory dishes, called for "blades of mace." That form of the spice is a lacy outer covering on the nutmeg shell. While I found it online, a jar of blades of mace is expensive and not widely available in stores. So instead, I used the ground form of mace, which is less expensive and more easily found in stores with large selections of spices. Another substitution was lamb for mutton. The cookbooks of Hamilton's era called for mutton, which is sheep at least one year old and typically three years old. Indeed, the records of Hamilton family purchases show they ate lots of mutton. However, mutton is no longer popular in the US and I could not find it, even from specialty butchers. Instead, I substituted lamb, which comes from sheep less than a year old.

In the case of measurements, if the dish yielded enough to serve a large crowd, I scaled it down. For example, the original gingerbread recipe serves about twenty. I halved that to make a large nine-inch (or twenty-three-centimeter cake), an ample size for eight to ten people.

Some measurements used in old recipes are easy to understand, but in a few cases, such as the strawberry water, the recipe is vague. The strawberry water recipe calls for a "pottle" of strawberries (a basket of varying size, holding anywhere from a quart to a pint of berries). I just had to guess at the amount of strawberries and the intensity of the desired strawberry flavor.

In the adapted recipes, why are two ingredients with the same volume measurement (e.g., teaspoons, cups) sometimes different weight measurements? How much space an ingredient takes up when measured (volume) is unrelated to how much that ingredient weighs. For example, a tablespoon of unsweetened cocoa weighs around 5 grams, while a tablespoon of sugar weighs about 12 grams. Keep in mind that a gram is quite a small amount (there are more than 28 grams in an ounce) and that different sources may provide slightly different measurements for the same amount of an ingredient. Depending on how you weigh all-purpose flour (e.g., sifted vs. unsifted, spoon-and-sweep vs. dipped) a one cup measurement in grams can vary from 120 to 142 grams.

How did you pick the recipes that are in this book?

I looked for recipes representing a variety of foods that the Hamiltons ate (or might well have eaten) and that would appeal to modern readers. There were lots of recipes from which to choose, so when it came down to deciding between several similar recipes, or deciding which vegetables to include, that was decidedly unscientific. I am not a picky eater and I love trying new recipes, so the choices between recipes were sometimes hard to make.

But, just like my own mother never made us eggplant when we were kids because she didn't like

it, when in doubt, I went with my taste buds. That meant that I chose bread pudding over rice pudding and hoe cakes over porridge. For one recipe choice, I owe a hat tip to my son, Liam, who lives in Philadelphia. Once, when chatting about my progress on the book, he asked whether Pepper Pot Soup would be included. Knowing nothing about that soup, I began to research its origins and components. Once I understood Pepper Pot's connection to the West Indies as well as Philadelphia, it was obvious that it deserved a place among my Hamilton-era recipes.

How can I find other recipes from Hamilton's era?

Numerous cookbooks from Hamilton's time and other time periods are digitized online. Three great sources for those digitized editions are the digitized materials from the Katharine Golden Bitting Collection of publications and gastronomy at: loc.gov/rr/rarebook/coll/028.html, the Joseph and Elizabeth Robins Pennell Collection of graphic arts, papers, and cookbooks at loc.gov/rr/print/coll/183.html, both at the US Library of Congress, and the HathiTrust Digital Library at hathitrust.org.

Chapter 6

Original & Adapted Recipes

Recipe Contents

Breakfast & Breads

A Nice Indian Pudding.

No. 1. 3 pints scalded milk, 7 spoons fine Indian meal, stir well together while hot, let stand till cooled; add 7 eggs, half pound raisins, 4 ounces butter, spice and sugar, bake one and half hour.

No. 2. 3 pints scalded milk to one pint meal salted; cool, add 2 eggs, 4 ounces butter, sugar or molasses and spice q. s. it will require two and half hours baking.

No. 3. Salt a pint meal, wet with one quart milk, sweeten and put into a strong cloth, brass or bell metal vessel, stone or earthern pot, secure from wet and boil 12 hours.

A Sunderland Pudding.

Whip 6 eggs, half the whites, take half a nutmeg, one point cream and a little salt, 4 spoons fine flour, oil or butter pans, cups, or bowls, bake in a quick oven one hour. Eat with sweet sauce.

A Whitpot.

Cut half a loaf of bread in slices, pour thereon 2 quarts milk, 6 eggs, rose-water, nutmeg and half pound of sugar; put into a dish and cover with paste, No. 1. bake slow 1 hour.

A Bread Pudding.

One pound soft bread or biscuit soaked in one quart milk, run thro' a sieve or cullender, add 7 eggs, three quarters of a pound sugar, one quarter of a pound butter, nutmeg or cinnamon, one gill rose-water, one pound stoned raisins, half pint cream, bake three quarters of an hour, middling oven.

A Flour Pudding.

Seven eggs, one quarter of a pound of sugar, and a tea spoon of salt, beat and put to one quart milk, 5 spoons of flour, cinnamon and nutmeg to your taste, bake half an hour, and serve up with sweet sauce.

A boiled Flour Pudding.

One quart milk, 9 eggs, 7 spoons flour, a little salt, put into a strong cloth and boiled three quarters of an hour.

Bread Pudding

Adapted from "A Bread Pudding," Amelia Simmons, *American Cookery*.

Serves 4 to 6

The better the bread, the better this bread pudding. I use a country white or sourdough with a nice crust. It puffs up slightly when baking, so if your casserole or soufflé dish is filled to the brim, put a cookie sheet underneath as it bakes, in order to avoid drips on the oven floor. Fabulous with a dollop of whipped cream or ice cream for dessert, this bread pudding is also delicious cold or re-heated for breakfast.

INGREDIENTS

½ pound crusty bread cut into small chunks
    (about ½- to 1-inch or cubes)

2 cups whole milk

4 large eggs

¾ cup granulated sugar

1½ cup raisins

½ cup heavy cream

1 teaspoon ground cinnamon

1 teaspoon rosewater or vanilla extract

4 tablespoons or ½ stick unsalted butter, cut into
    small pieces, plus more for buttering the dish

1. If the bread is not already stale: Preheat oven to 300°F. Put the bread cubes onto a cookie sheet and bake until they are no longer soft. Typically, this step takes 15 or more minutes, depending on how stale the bread is at the beginning.

2. Increase the oven temperature to 350°F.

3. Butter a two-quart casserole or soufflé dish, and set aside.

4. Put the bread cubes and milk in a large bowl. Let the mixture stand until the bread soaks up most or all of the liquid.

5. Add all remaining ingredients except the butter. Stir until combined.

6. Pour the ingredients into the prepared casserole and dot it with the butter. Let the unbaked bread pudding stand on the counter at least 20 minutes, to give the mixture time to soak into the bread.

7. Put a cookie sheet underneath the casserole (to catch any drips) and bake the bread pudding for about 45 to 60 minutes, until a knife inserted in the middle comes out clean.

8. Let the bread pudding cool down for at least 15 to 20 minutes before serving.

Chardoons *fry'd and buttered.*

YOU muſt cut them about ten Inches, and ſtring them, t tye them up in Bundles like Aſparagus, or cut them in ſ Dice, boil them like Peas, toſs them up with Pepper, Salt, melted Butter.

Chardoons a la Framage.

AFTER they are ſtringed, cut them an Inch long, ſtew th in a little Red Wine till they are tender, ſeaſon with Pep and Salt, and thicken it with a Piece of Butter rolled in Flo then pour them into your Diſh, ſqueeze the Juice of Orange o it, then ſcrape *Cheſhire* Cheeſe all over them, then brown it w a Cheeſe Iron, and ſerve it up quick and hot.

To make a Scotch Rabbit.

TOAST a Piece of Bread very nicely on both Sides, butter cut a Slice of Cheeſe about as big as the Bread, toaſt i both Sides, and lay it on the Bread.

To make a Welch Rabbit.

TOAST the Bread on both Sides, then toaſt the Cheeſe one Side, lay it on the Toaſt, and with a hot Iron brown other Side. You may rub it over with Muſtard.

To make an Engliſh Rabbit.

TOAST a Slice of Bread brown on both Sides, then lay a Plate before the Fire, pour a Glaſs of Red Wine over and let it ſoak the Wine up; then cut ſome Cheeſe very thin, lay it very thick over the Bread; put it in a Tin Oven before Fire, and it will be toaſted and brown preſently. Serve it a hot.

Or do it thus.

TOAST the Bread and ſoak it in the Wine, ſet it before Fire, cut your Cheeſe in very thin Slices, rub Butter over Bottom of a Plate, lay the Cheeſe on, pour in two or three Sp fuls of White Wine, cover it with another Plate, ſet it ov Chafing-diſh of hot Coals for two or three Minutes, then ſtir i it is done and well mixed. You may ſtir in a little Muſt when it is enough lay it on the Bread, juſt brown it with a Shovel. Serve it away hot.

S

Toaster Oven English Rabbit

Adapted from "To Make an English Rabbit," Hannah Glasse, *The Art of Cookery Made Plain and Easy.*

Serves 1

Rarebit (or rabbit in the original spelling) is toasted bread with melted cheese. Hannah Glasse had three versions: Scotch (plain), Welch (with mustard), and English (with red wine). This English Rabbit is like a spiked cheese fondue without having to fuss with a fondue pot. If you're scaling the recipe to serve more than 2 people, you may want to use a larger ("regular") oven in order to bake all the slices of bread at once.

INGREDIENTS

2 small or 1 large thick slice of crusty country white
   or sourdough bread
2 to 3 ounces dry red wine
1½ to 2 ounces sharp cheddar cheese, grated
   or thinly sliced
Oil, optional

1. Toast the bread. Once you remove it from the toaster oven, turn the oven to a bake setting and preheat at 350°F.
2. Put the bread in a wide-bottomed bowl or a plate with sides and pour the wine over it. Let the bread sit in the wine until all of the liquid is absorbed.
3. Either oil the bottom of the toaster oven pan or line it with foil. Place the wine-soaked bread on the pan and top with the cheese. Bake until the cheese bubbles.
4. Serve the toasted bread hot.

Johny Cake, or Hoe Cake.

Scald 1 pint of milk and put to 3 pints of indian meal, and half pint of flower—bake before the fire. Or scald with milk two thirds of the indian meal, or wet two thirds with boiling water, add salt, molasses and shortening, work up with cold water pretty stiff, and bake as above.

Indian Slapjack.

One quart of milk, 1 pint of indian meal, 4 eggs, 4 spoons of flour, little salt, beat together, baked on gridles, or fry in a dry pan, or baked in a pan which has been rub'd with suet, lard or butter.

Loaf Cakes.

No. 1. Rub 6 pound of sugar, 2 pound of lard, 3 pound of butter into 12 pound of flour, add 18 eggs, 1 quart of milk, 2 ounces of cinnamon, 2 small nutmegs, a tea cup of coriander seed, each pounded fine and sifted, add one pint of brandy, half a pint of wine, 6 pound of stoned raisins, 1 pint of emptins, first having dried your flour in the oven, dry and roll the sugar fine, rub your shortning and sugar half an hour, it will render the cake much whiter and lighter, heat the oven with dry wood, for 1 and a half hours, if large pans be used, it will then require 2 hours baking, and in proportion for smaller loaves. To frost it. Whip 6 whites, during the baking, add 3 pound of sifted loaf sugar and put on thick, as it comes hot from the oven. Some return the frosted loaf into the oven, it injures and yellows it, if the frosting be put on immediately it does best without being returned into the oven.

Another.

No. 2. Rub 4 pound of sugar, 3 and a half pound of shortning, (half butter and half lard) into 9 pound of flour, 1 dozen of eggs, 2 ounces of cinnamon, 1 pint of milk, 3 spoonfuls coriander seed, 3 gills of brandy, 1 gill of wine, 3 gills of emptins, 4 pounds of raisins.

Johnny or Hoe Cakes

Adapted from "Johny Cake, or Hoe Cake,"
Amelia Simmons, *American Cookery*.

Serves about 12
(2- to 3-inch patties)

These Johnny (Johny) or Hoe Cakes do not have leavening. As a result, they are stiffer and heavier than modern pancakes. The molasses makes them slightly sweet. You can eat them with your hands. I dipped them in maple syrup for a snack. Increasing the liquid (milk) to a 1-to-1 ratio of cornmeal to liquid yields a thinner, more pancake-like patty.

INGREDIENTS

2 cups cornmeal
½ teaspoon kosher or sea salt
1 cup milk, scalded (heated almost to boiling
    and then cooled slightly)
2 tablespoons unsalted butter, melted
2 tablespoons molasses
Vegetable oil for frying

1. Mix the salt into the cornmeal in a medium bowl, and set aside.
2. Add the melted butter and the molasses to the scalded milk and mix well until the molasses dissolves in the hot liquid.
3. Add the liquid ingredients to the cornmeal mixture. Mix well and let stand for 1 to 2 minutes. Then add cold water by tablespoonsful, probably 2 to 3 tablespoons will suffice, until the mixture is pliable but still stiff enough to form by hand into patties about ¼- to ½-inch thick.
4. Heat a heavy pan, preferably cast iron. Add the vegetable oil, then put the 4 to 6 patties into the pan. Cook about 3 minutes until the patties are well browned, then flip them and fry their other side. Repeat with any remaining batter.
5. Serve immediately.

Soups

of celery, six or eight onions, four turneps and a ca
rot, four cloves and two blades of mace, sweat it ov
a gentle fire for half an hour; in the mean time b
two quarts of old green peas well, and strain the liqu
into your pot, and when it boils skim it well; boil
gently till it is good, strain it off into a pan, beat t
peas well in a mortar, and mix the soup with the
and rub it through a tammy or napkin; if you have
mortar, you may rub the peas through a sieve with t
back of a spoon, and mix with your soup; put it in
your pot again, pare two or three cucumbers, cut the
down the middle, take out the pulp, and cut them
inch long, four cabbage lettuces cut across, boil the
till tender, and a pint of young peas boiled green, p
them into your soup and boil it up for five minute
season it with pepper and salt to your palate: if yo
find your soup not thick enough, take the crumb of
French roll, put a little soup to it, and simmer it, th
rub it as the peas and put it in, stir it well about, an
two or three minutes before you send it away put in ha
a pint of spinach juice, and keep it stirring till it bo
up, just to take the rawness of the spinach off; the
put it in tureens, and send crispt bread in a plate.

N. B. You may stew a little spinach and squeeze
dry, chop it a little and put it in with the peas, &c.

Another Green Peas Soup.

TAKE a gallon of spring water and make it bo
then put in two quarts of old green peas, and bo
them till tender, strain them off and save the liquo
and put it in the pot again, with six or eight larg
onions, six turneps, two carrots, six heads of celer
and if you have them six cabbage lettuces, a little sp
nach, all well washed, a little cloves and mace; bo
them till all are tender, beat your old peas well in
mortar and mix with the soup, and rub it all we
through a tammy or napkin; put it in your pot agai
season it with pepper and salt to your palate, then tre
it as in the above receipt.

Split Pea Soup

Adapted from "Another Green Peas Soup," Richard Briggs, *The English Art of Cookery*.

Serves 8

This mildly seasoned vegetarian pea soup is thick and hearty, a perfect supper for a chilly evening. Hamilton's family would probably have served a version with meat in the Dutch tradition. (Elizabeth Hamilton's family was of Dutch origin and highly influenced by the Dutch traditions that remained prevalent around their Albany home.) The Dutch version, called erwtensoep or snert, typically includes pork products such as a Dutch sausage called rookworst. Instead of croutons, they might have had rye bread topped with Dutch-style smoked bacon.

INGREDIENTS

2¼ cups or 1 pound dried split green peas

3 medium-large onions (about 1 to 1½ pounds), peeled and chopped

1 or 2 small-medium turnips (about ½ to 1 pound), peeled and chopped

1 large carrot (about 3 to 4 ounces), peeled and chopped

3 cabbage leaves, coarsely cut

1 handful of spinach leaves, tough stems removed

½ teaspoon ground mace

2 pinches ground cloves

2 teaspoons kosher or sea salt

Freshly ground black pepper

Croutons

1. Boil 2 quarts (8 cups) of water. Add the split peas and simmer about 1 hour or until the peas are tender and fully cooked.

2. Add 1 to 2 more cups of water. Bring the peas and liquid to a boil. Add the vegetables, mace, and cloves. Cover and simmer about 15 minutes, until the vegetables are tender. Season with the salt and pepper.

3. Purée the soup in a stand blender or with an immersion blender, and adjust seasonings to taste. If the soup is too thick for your taste, add a bit more water.

4. Serve topped with croutons.

brisket and take the bones out, keep it hot, strain your soup into a pan to settle, skim off all the fat, and pour it from the settlings into a soup-pot, put in two spoonfuls of browning, cut a carrot, two turneps, two leeks, and four heads of celery in long slips, and boil them in your soup till tender; then put the brisket into a tureen or soup-dish, and pour the soup over it, with crispt bread in a plate.

Soup and Boulée with Cabbage.

TAKE six pounds of brisket of beef, tie it up with two pounds of scrag of veal, put them into a pot with six quarts of water, and when the scum rises skim it well, and boil it gently for two hours; cut two carrots in quarters, four turneps in quarters, two leeks split in two, and four heads of celery, cut one large or two small cabbages in quarters and across about an inch long, wash them all well, put them in with a bundle of sweet herbs, some all-spice, cloves, and mace tied in a bag, season it with salt, and boil it gently for three hours longer; skim the fat off well and take the brisket out, untie it and put it in a dish by itself, and garnish it with carrot; take out the veal, spices, and herbs, and put the soup and the ingredients into a tureen, with crispt bread in a plate.

A West-India Pepper Pot.

TAKE two pounds of lean veal, the same of mutton, cut them small, with a pound of lean ham, put them in a stew-pan, and about four pounds of brisket of beef cut in square pieces, with six onions, two carrots, four heads of celery, four leeks, two turneps, well washed, a bundle of sweet herbs, some all-spice, cloves, and mace, and half a pint of water; sweat them well for half an hour, then pour four quarts of boiling water into it, and skim it well; boil it gently for three hours, then strain it off, take out the pieces of beef; then put a quarter of a pound of butter in the stew-pan and melt it, put two spoonfuls of flour, and stir it about till it is smooth; then by degrees pour your soup in,

in, and stir it about to keep it from lumping, put the pieces of beef in; have ready two large carrots cut in quarters, and four turneps in quarters, boiled till tender, take the spawn of a large lobster and bruise it fine, and put it in to colour it, with a dozen heads of greens boiled tender; make some flour and water into a paste, and make it in balls as big as a walnut, boil them well in water, and put them in; boil it up gently for fifteen minutes, and season it very hot with Cayan pepper and salt; put it in a soup-dish and send it up hot, garnished with sprigs of cauliflowers round the dish, or carrots, or any thing else you fancy.

Hare Soup.

TAKE a large old hare and cut it in pieces, put it in an earthen mug, with three or four blades of mace, a little salt and Cayan pepper, two large onions, a red herring, six large morels, a pint of red wine, and three quarts of water; tie it down with brown paper, bake it three hours in a quick oven, then strain it into a pan and let it settle; pour it from the settlings into a stew-pan, scald the liver for two or three minutes, and rub it through a sieve with a spoon and put it in; have ready a quarter of a pound of French barley, boiled well in water, and put in, put it over the fire to make hot, (but take care it does not boil) then pour it into a soup-dish or tureen, with crispt French bread at the top. This is esteemed as a very rich soup, and fit for a large company, where two or three soups are served up.

N. B. If you disapprove of the red herring you may leave it out.

Partridge Soup.

TAKE two old partridges and skin them, cut them into quarters, with three or four slices of ham, six onions sliced, and four heads of celery; fry them brown in butter, but do not burn them, pour three quarts of boiling water over them, with a few pepper corns, and stew it gently for two hours; take out the partridges

West Indian Pepper Pot Soup

Adapted from "A West-India Pepper Pot," Richard Briggs, *The English Art of Cookery*.

Serves 8 to 10

This soup, popular both in the West Indies and in the Philadelphia area, is a mélange of many ingredients and spices. The taste is complex and exotic.

INGREDIENTS

2 to 4 tablespoons olive or other oil, divided
1 pound veal or veal sausage, cut into pieces
½ pound cooked ham, cut into pieces
1 lamb chop, about 4 to 5 ounces, cut into chunks
2 pounds stew beef (chuck roast or similar cut),
    cut into chunks if it is not pre-cut
3 medium onions, peeled and chopped
2 stalks celery, chopped
1 large or 2 small leeks, cleaned and chopped
    (white to light green parts only)
1 tablespoon fresh thyme leaves
    or 1 teaspoon dried thyme
1½ teaspoons fresh rosemary leaves
    or ½ teaspoon dried rosemary leaves
2 bay leaves
3 cloves
Freshly ground black pepper
¼ teaspoon ground allspice
¼ teaspoon ground mace
1 large carrot, cut into chunks
1 small-medium turnip, cut into chunks
6 leaves of cabbage, thinly sliced into ribbons
a 6-ounce can of crabmeat, drained
Cayenne pepper or dried red pepper flakes, to taste
2 tablespoons unsalted butter
2¼ cups (or more all-purpose flour, divided
¾ teaspoon kosher or sea salt (for dumplings),
    plus more for soup if desired

1. Heat 1 to 2 tablespoons of oil and brown the meats in a large pan, in batches if necessary. Remove the meat to a bowl, and set aside.
2. Add the remaining oil to a pan; on medium heat, cook the onion, celery, and leeks a few minutes until they release their juices. Add the herbs and spices and continue cooking for 3 to 4 minutes.
3. Put the onions, celery, leeks, and meats (except the crab) in a very large pot, add 2 quarts of boiling water and cook, skimming the foam off the soup while simmering it for 1½ to 2 hours.
4. In a small saucepan, melt the butter and 2 tablespoons flour. Stir together until fully mixed (forming a roux) and cook 1 to 2 minutes, stirring continuously. Add the roux to the soup and stir until the roux is fully incorporated, then add the carrot, turnip, cabbage, and canned crab. Bring the soup to a simmer.
5. For the dumplings: Mix the salt and remaining 2 cups of flour in a medium-sized deep bowl. Slowly add ¾ to 1 cup water and mix until the dough is wet but not runny. Form walnut-sized pieces (I use a spoon) from the dough and drop them into the simmering soup. Cover and cook the dumplings 15 to 20 minutes, then immediately serve the soup.

Fish & Seafood

Baked Whole Whitefish

Adapted from "To bake a Turbot," Hannah Glasse,
The Art of Cookery Made Plain and Easy.

Serves 2

*This recipe, originally written for turbot (a flat
fish similar to flounder), works well with any
similar-sized white, mild, and flaky whitefish
(e.g., black bass, branzino, or trout). When Hannah
Glasse adds "catchup" to the sauce, she is not
referring to the spicy-sweet tomato sauce we call
ketchup. Instead, she probably meant a thick
anchovy- or mushroom-based condiment. She
suggests serving this fish cold, but I prefer it hot.*

INGREDIENTS

Whole, mild whitefish about 2½ to 3 pounds, scaled,
    gutted, and fins removed. Optional: Ask the fish
    store to remove the head and tail. Depending on
    the type of fish, you may need two smaller fish,
    each 1¼ to 1½ pounds.
1 cup dry white wine (enough to go about ¾ of
    the way up the fish when it is placed in the pan),
    plus a splash for sauce
1 tablespoon minced parsley
1½ tablespoons unsalted butter, divided
1 tablespoon all-purpose flour
¼ teaspoon ground nutmeg
½ teaspoon kosher or coarse sea salt
Freshly ground black pepper
½ cup breadcrumbs, slightly moistened with
    melted butter
Lemon slices

1. Preheat the oven to 425°F.
2. Place the whole prepared fish (minus head and
   tail) into a pan with high sides that is just large
   enough to fit the fish snugly. Pour 1 cup of the
   wine into the pan; add the parsley.
3. Dot the fish with 1 tablespoon of butter and
   sprinkle the flour over the top, along with the
   nutmeg, salt, and pepper. Add the breadcrumbs
   and bake 10 to 25 minutes or until the fish is fully
   cooked. (It should flake easily when you pick
   off a small piece with a fork.) The wide range of
   cooking times is due to the varied thicknesses
   of the fish. For thinner fish such as turbot and
   flounder, the baking time will be less; it will be
   longer for thicker fish such as bass, branzino,
   or trout.
4. Remove the fish and bring the pan drippings to
   the stovetop, either in the pan (if it is safe for
   stovetop cooking) or in a small saucepan. Add
   the remaining ½ tablespoon of butter and the
   splash of wine. Bring this small amount of sauce
   to a boil. Immediately pour it over the fish and
   serve with lemon slices.

To bake a Turbot.

Take a dish the size of your turbot, rub butter all over it thick, throw a little salt, a little beaten pepper, and half a large nutmeg, some parsley minced fine, and throw all over, pour in a pint of white-wine; cut off the head and tail, lay the turbot in the dish, pour another pint of white-wine all over, grate the other half of the nutmeg over it, and a little pepper, some salt and chopped parsley. Lay a piece of butter here and there all over, and throw a little flour all over, and then a good many crumbs of bread. Bake it, and be sure that it is of a fine brown; then lay it in your dish, stir the sauce in your dish all together, pour it into a sauce-pan, shake in a little flour, let it boil, then stir in a piece of butter and two spoonfuls of catchup, let it boil, and pour it into basons. Garnish your dish with lemon; and you may add what you fancy to the sauce, as shrimps, anchovies, mushrooms, &c. If a small turbout, half the wine will do. It eats finely thus. Lay it in a dish, skim off all the fat, and pour the rest over it. Let it stand till cold, and it is good with vinegar, and a fine dish to set out a cold table.

To broil Salmon.

Cut fresh salmon into thick pieces, flour them and broil them, lay them in your dish, and have plain melted butter in a cup.

Baked Samon.

Take a little piece cut into slices about an inch thich, butter the dish that you would serve it to table on, lay the slices in the dish, take off the skin, make a force-meat thus: take the flesh of an eel, the flesh of a salmon an equal quantity, beat in a mortar, season it with beaten pepper, salt, bread, beat up one yolk of an egg with one spoonful of vinegar, throw it in, then shake the sauce pan round a minute, and serve it up on a plate.

To stew Prawns, Shrimps, or Craw-Fish.

Pick out the tail, lay them by, about two quarts; take the bodies, give them a bruise, and put them into a pint of white-wine, with a blade of mace; let them stew a quarter of an hour, stir them together, and strain them; then wash out the saucepan, put to it the strained liquor and tails: grate a small nutmeg in, add a little salt, and a quarter of a pound of butter rolled in flour: shake it all together; cut a pretty thin toast round a quartern loaf toast it brown on both sides, cut into six pieces, lay it close together in the bottom of your dish, and pour your fish and sauce over it. Send it to table hot. If it be craw-fish or prawns, garnish your dish with some of the biggest claws laid thick round. Water will do in the room of wine, only add a spoonful of vinegar.

To make Scollops of Oysters.

Put your oysters into scollop-shells for that purpose, set them on your gridiron over a good clear fire, let them stew till you think your oysters are enough, then have ready some crumbs of bread rubbed in a clean napkin, fill your shells, and set them before a good fire, and baste them well with butter. Let them be of a fine brown, keeping them turning, to be brown all over alike: but a tin oven does them best before the fire. They eat much the best done this way, though most people stew the oysters first in a sauce-pan, with a blade of mace, thickened with a piece of butter, and fill the shells, and then cover them with crumbs, and brown them with a hot iron: but the bread has not the fine taste of the former.

Scalloped Oysters

Adapted from "To make Scollops of Oysters," Hannah Glasse, *The Art of Cookery Made Plain and Easy.*

Serves 2 as a main course, or 4 as an appetizer or side dish

This simple dish consists of baked oysters and a crunchy breadcrumb topping. The flavors of the oysters and the buttery topping shine without seasoning. If you prefer a more seasoned version, add a bit of Dijon mustard to the liquid or serve the dish with hot sauce on the side.

INGREDIENTS

½ cup fresh breadcrumbs, preferably from
    a baguette or other bread with a crispy crust
½ cup Panko breadcrumbs
⅛ teaspoon kosher or sea salt
Freshly ground black pepper
3 tablespoons butter, melted
1 pint (1 pound) shucked oysters,
    including their juices
2 tablespoons whole milk, half-and-half,
    or heavy cream

1. Preheat the oven to 400°F.
2. Mix both styles of breadcrumbs, salt, pepper, and butter in a small bowl.
3. Spread the oysters with their juices in an ovenproof dish just large enough to contain the oysters in a single layer. (A casserole dish about 5 × 7½-inches works well.) Note: If the oysters you use are already shucked in a jar, make sure the liquid is all oyster "juice." If the jar indicates that it includes water, add only a few tablespoons of the liquid—not all of it. The oysters should be barely wet with juices.
4. Add the milk, half-and-half, or cream, and stir just enough to make sure that the oyster juices and the dairy are combined.
5. Top with the breadcrumb mixture and bake 20 to 25 minutes, until the breadcrumbs are golden brown. If the breadcrumbs brown too quickly, once they are golden, cover the casserole lightly with aluminum foil and continue cooking.
6. Serve immediately.

Meats

Note, When you do it in a Pewter Dish, it is best done on Chaffing-dish of hot Coals, with a Bit or two of Charcoal to it alive.

Beef *Escarlot.*

TAKE a Brisquit of Beef, Half a Pound of coarse Sugar, Ounces of Bay Salt, a Pound of common Salt, mix all ther and rub the Beef, lay it in an earthen Pan, and turn it e Day, It may lie a Fortnight in the Pickle, then boil it, and it up either with Savoys, or a Pease Pudding.

Note, It eats much finer cold, cut into Slices, and sent to T

Beef *à la Daub.*

YOU may take a Buttock or a Rump of Beef, lard it, Brown in some sweet Butter, then put it into a Pot that just hold it; put in some Broth or Gravy hot, some Pep Cloves, Mace, and a Bundle of Sweet Herbs, stew it four H till it is tender, and season it with Salt; take Half a Pint of vy, two Sweetbreads cut into eight Pieces, some Truffles and rels, Palates, Artichoke-Bottoms and Mushrooms, boil all t ther, lay your Beef into the Dish, strain the Liqour into the S and boil all together. If it is not thick enough roll a Piece of ter in Flour, and boil in it. Pour this all over the Beef. T Force-Meat roll'd in Pieces Half as long as one's Finger, dip t into Batter made with Eggs, and fry them Brown, fry some pets dipp'd into Batter cut three Corner ways, stick them into Meat, and garnish with the Force-Meat.

Beef *à la Mode in Pieces.*

YOU must take a Buttock of Beef, cut it into two Pound Pie lard them with Bacon, fry them Brown, put them into a that will just hold them, put in two Quarts of Broth or Grav few Sweet Herbs, an Onion, some Mace, Cloves, Nutmeg, per and Salt; when that is done, cover it close, and stew till tender, skim off all the Fat, lay the Meat in the Dish, and the Sauce over it. You may serve it up hot or cold.

Beef *à la Mode, the French Way.*

TAKE a Piece of the Buttock of Beef, and some fat Bacon into little long Bits, then take two Tea Spoonfuls of Salt, Tea Spoonful of beaten Pepper, one of beaten Mace, and on Nutmeg; mix all together, have your Larding-pins ready, dip the Bacon in Vinegar, then roll it in your Spice, and

Beef à la Mode

Adapted from "Beef à la Mode in Pieces," Hannah Glasse, *The Art of Cookery Made Plain and Easy*.

Serves 6 to 8

This recipe is what I call pot roast. The gravy is rather thin (because it has no flour or other thickener), but flavorful. Adding carrot, potato, turnip, and/or parsnip chunks cooked separately or added during the last 20 to 30 minutes of simmering, turns this dish into an appetizing one-pot dinner. The original recipe calls for multiple two-pound pieces of meat, hence the name "in Pieces." This adaptation makes a smaller amount, with a single piece of meat roughly that size.

INGREDIENTS

3 to 4 strips bacon, cut into triangles 1 to 2 inches long and about 1 inch wide, with a point at one end. Freeze until the bacon triangles are hard.

Stewing beef such as chuck roast, roughly 2 to 3 pounds

2 tablespoons olive oil

1 quart beef broth or stock

1 medium onion, peeled and thinly sliced

¼ teaspoon ground mace

2 whole cloves or ¼ teaspoon ground cloves

¼ teaspoon ground nutmeg

Kosher or sea salt

Freshly ground black pepper

1. Cut tiny slits in the meat about every two inches, and insert the frozen bacon triangles, pointy end first. Work them all the way into the meat. They will soften and cook along with the meat.

2. Heat the olive oil in a Dutch oven or other heavy pot that is just about the size of the beef. Sear the meat on all sides. Add the broth or stock, onion slices, mace, cloves, and nutmeg. Cover the pot and bring the liquid to a boil, then reduce the heat until the liquid is at a simmer. Simmer for about 1½ to 1¾ hours, then add salt and pepper to taste. Continue cooking until the beef is tender, about 15 to 30 minutes longer.

3. Skim off the fat or use a fat separator, remove the onion, and strain the liquid. Note: An easy way to skim fat if you are not serving the meat immediately is to refrigerate the meat and gravy until the fat congeals, then scrape it off with a spoon. The beef and strained "sauce" may be reheated or the beef may be served cold or room temperature with room temperature sauce.

skin, then set them on in cold water, and let them simmer till they begin to be tender; take them out and flour them, and broil them on the gridiron. In the mean time take a little good gravy, a little mustard, a little bit of butter rolled in flour, give it a boil, season it with pepper and salt. Lay the sounds in your dish and pour your sauce over them.

Fried Sausages.

Take half a pound of sausages, and six apples, slice four about as thick as a crown, cut the other two in quarters, fry them with the sausages of a fine light brown, lay the sausages in the middle of the dish, and the apples round. Garnish with the quartered apples.

Stewed cabbage and sausages fried is a good dish; then heat cold peas-pudding in the pan, lay it in the dish and the sausages round, heap the pudding in the middle, and lay the sausages all round thick up, edge-ways, and one in the middle at length.

Collops and Eggs.

Cut either bacon, pickled beef, or hung mutton, into thin slices, broil them nicely, lay them in a dish before the fire, have ready a stew-pan of water boiling, break as many eggs as you have collops, break them one by one in a cup, and pour them into the stew-pan. When the whites of the eggs begin to harden, and all look of a clear white, take them up one by one in an egg-slice, and lay them on the collops.

To dress cold Fowl or Pigeon.

Cut them in four quarters, beat up an egg or two according to what you dress, grate a little nutmeg in, a little salt, some parsley chopped, a few crumbs of bread; beat them well together, dip them in this batter, and have ready some dripping hot in a

Fried Sausages and Apples

Adapted from "Fried Sausages," Hannah Glasse,
The Art of Cookery Made Plain and Easy.

Serves 2 (as a main dish)

This dish is great for a weeknight dinner; it is quick to prepare and uses just one large pan. It makes a full meal with just a salad and a loaf of crusty bread.

INGREDIENTS

½ to ¾ pound thick country or other similarly spiced chicken, turkey, or pork sausage (about 1-inch in diameter)

4 to 6 apples, preferably of mixed varieties, peeled and quartered. Any apples that keep their shape will work (e.g., Granny Smith, Yellow and Red Delicious, and Fuji). Quarter, and thinly slice half of the quartered apples.

1. In a large, heavy pan, start the sausages cooking under medium-high heat. As soon as the sausages begin to render their juices, add the thin apple slices. Turn both the sausages and the apple slices so that they brown evenly.

2. Once the apple slices begin to brown, add the apple quarters, and stir occasionally. After 2 to 3 minutes, cover the pan for a few minutes. That helps the apples soften and brown. It will also allow a bit of liquid to accumulate in the pan. Uncover the pan and continue cooking until the sausages are fully cooked. (The time required to cook the sausages depends on their thickness, typically about 10 to 15 minutes. You can ensure that the middle cooks thoroughly by cutting the sausages down the middle vertically to butterfly them after 10 minutes, laying them flat to continue cooking for another 3 to 5 minutes.) The thin apple slices will slightly disintegrate into a chunky applesauce, while the quarters will remain whole.

3. Serve on a platter with the sausages in the middle along with the applesauce, surrounded by the apple quarters.

Lamb Stew

Adapted from "A Harrico of Mutton," Hannah Glasse, *The Art of Cookery Made Plain and Easy.*

Serves 6 to 8

This stew is a tasty, one-dish meal, with a light broth. The original recipe calls for mutton, but it is difficult to find in North America. Lamb is meat from a sheep less than one year old. Stronger tasting and tougher than lamb, mutton is from an animal older than one year, and typically about three years old. Using lamb that is intended for stewing (from the neck, shoulder, or breast) approximates the consistency of mutton. While the flavor may not be as strong as mutton, stewing lamb still has a markedly different taste than beef.

INGREDIENTS

3 pounds of boneless lamb stew meat (from the neck, shoulder, or breast) cut into 2-inch cubes. (If you buy lamb on the bone and cube it yourself, count on about 4¾ pounds of bone-in meat.)

½ cup all-purpose flour

3 tablespoons unsalted butter, oil, or a combination

¼ teaspoon ground mace

1 tablespoon fresh thyme leaves or 1 teaspoon dried leaves

1 bay leaf

12 chestnuts, blanched if fresh, or jarred (already blanched)

½ teaspoon kosher or sea salt, plus more to taste

Freshly ground black pepper

1 to 2 small-medium turnips (about 8 ounces), peeled and cut into chunks

3 medium carrots (about 8 ounces), peeled and cut into chunks

2 to 3 leaves Romaine lettuce or white cabbage, shredded or cut into small pieces

6 pearl onions (the small boiling type)

1. Put the flour into a plastic bag. Add the cubed lamb and shake until all the meat is well covered with flour. Shake off the excess flour and set the lamb cubes aside.

2. Heat the butter or oil in a heavy skillet and sear the lamb cubes on all sides. Transfer them to a heavy pot. Add the ground mace and the herbs, chestnuts, and 2 cups of water.

3. Cover and let the meat and chestnuts simmer for 1 hour. Drain off the fat. (If you're making the stew at least a few hours before serving, or the previous day, remove the fat by refrigerating the stew, then spooning off the solidified fat before adding the vegetables.)

4. Add the salt and pepper, to taste, and vegetables; cook about 15 minutes until the carrots and turnips are softened.

To *Roast* a Leg of Mutton *with* Oysters.

TAKE a Leg about two or three Days kill'd, stuff it all over with Oysters, and roast it. Garnish with Horse-raddish.

To *Roast* a Leg of Mutton *with* Cockles.

STUFF it all over with Cockles, and roast it. Garnish with Horse-raddish.

A Shoulder of Mutton *in Epigram.*

ROAST it almost enough, then very carefully take off the Skin about the Thickness of a Crown-piece, and the Shank Bone with it at the End, then season that Skin and Shank Bone with Pepper and Salt, a little Lemon-peel cut small, and a few Sweet Herbs and Crumbs of Bread, then lay this on the Gridiron, and let it be of a fine Brown; in the mean Time take the rest of the Meat and cut it like a Hash about the Bigness of a Shilling, save the Gravy and put to it, with a few Spoonfuls of strong Gravy, Half an Onion cut fine, a little Nutmeg, a little Pepper and Salt, a little Bundle of Sweet Herbs, some Gerkins cut very small, a few Mushrooms, two or three Truffles cut small, two Spoonfuls of Wine, either Red or White, and throw a little Flour over the Meat; let all these stew together very softly for five or six Minutes, but be sure it don't boil, take out the Sweet Herbs, and put the Hash into the Dish, lay the Broil'd upon it, and send it to Table.

A *Harrico of* Mutton.

TAKE a Neck or Loin of Mutton, cut it into six Pieces, flour it, and fry it Brown on both Sides in the Stew-pan, then pour out all the Fat, put in some Turnips and Carrots cut like Dice, two Dozen of Chesnuts blanched, two or three Lettuces cut small, six little round Onions, a Bundle of Sweet Herbs, some Pepper and Salt, and two or three Blades of Mace; cover it close, and let it stew for an Hour, then take off the Fat and dish it up.

To French *a* Hind Saddle of Mutton.

IT is the two Rumps. Cut off the Rump, and carefully lift up the Skin with a Knife, begin at the broad End, but be sure you don't crack it nor take it quite off, then take some Slices of Ham or Bacon chopp'd fine, a few Truffles, some young Onions, some Parsley, a little Thyme, Sweet Marjoram, Winter Savoury,

a little

Slow Cooker Corned Beef

Adapted from "To Stew Brisket of Beef," Briggs, *The English Art of Cookery*.

Serves 4 to 6

Like the original version, this recipe uses beef preserved by corning. However, it begins with an already corned piece of brisket, commonly available in modern grocery stores. If you would like to corn your own brisket from scratch, here two resources on how to do that:

> simplyrecipes.com/recipes/home_cured
> _corned_beef

> ruhlman.com/2010/03/corned-beef-how-to
> -cure-your-own

INGREDIENTS

Corned beef brisket (about 3 pounds) Note: If your brisket comes with a package of pickling spices, this recipe does not use it.

3 to 4 shallots, peeled, halved if large, or 1 large red or sweet onion, peeled and cut into crescents or chunks

1 teaspoon black peppercorns

1 to 2 large sprigs fresh thyme or 1 teaspoon dried thyme

¼ teaspoon freshly grated nutmeg or ¼ teaspoon plus 1 to 2 extra pinches of ground nutmeg

two 12-ounce bottles or cans of beer (preferably a lager, which is crisper and less fruity than ale)

3 to 4 medium turnips (about 1½ pounds), peeled and cut into large chunks

4 to 5 medium yellow potatoes (about 1½ pounds), cut into large chunks

DRESSING/GRAVY (Optional)

1 tablespoon cornstarch mixed with 1 tablespoon cold water for each cup of cooking liquid
OR
2 tablespoons unsalted butter, melted, whisked with 2 tablespoons all-purpose flour for each cup of cooking liquid

To Make the Corned Beef

1. Rinse the corned beef and place it fat side up in a large (5 to 6 ½ quart) slow cooker. Place the shallots or onion around the meat, and add the peppercorns, thyme, and nutmeg. Pour the beer over the meat, plus enough water as needed to just cover the meat. Cook on high for 4½ to 5½ hours or 8 to10 hours on low.

2. Add the turnips and potatoes when about 1 hour is left on the cooking time on high or 1½ to 2½ hours is left if cooking on low.

To Make the Dressing/Gravy

The cooking liquid is light and aromatic. Strain it through a small strainer, taste, and use on the side as-is if it suits you. For a slightly more syrupy and less aromatic dressing, strain 1 cup of the liquid, add 1 tablespoon cornstarch mixed with 1 table-spoon of cold water, and stir the mixture in a small pot on medium heat until it thickens slightly. For a rich, thicker gravy, melt 2 tablespoons butter in a small pot, and let it foam, then brown slightly. When the foam dies down, add 2 tablespoons of flour and whisk the mixture, cooking the flour on medium-low about 2 minutes. Slowly add 1 cup of the strained liquid, whisking constantly, and cook until it thickens to your satisfaction.

To Stew Brisket of Beef.

Having rubbed the brisket with common salt and saltpetre, let it lie four days. Then lard the skin with fat bacon, and put it into a stew pan with a quart of water; a pint of red wine, or strong beer, half a pound of butter, a bunch of sweet herbs, three or four shallots, some pepper and half a nutmeg grated. Cover the pan very close. Stew it over a gentle fire for six hours. Then fry some square pieces of boiled turnips very brown. Strain the liquor the beef was stewed in, thicken it with burnt butter, and having mixed the turnips with it, pour all together over the beef in a large dish. Serve it up hot, and garnish with lemon sliced. An ox cheek or a leg of beef, may be served up in the same manner.

To Stew Beef Gobbets.

Cut any piece of beef, except the leg, in pieces, the size of a pullet's egg. Put them into a stew pan, and cover them with water. Let them stew one hour and skim them very clean. Then add a sufficient quantity of mace, cloves, and whole pepper, tied up loose in a muslin rag, some celery cut small, and salt, turnips, and carrots, pared and cut in slices, a little parsley, a bundle of sweet herbs, a large crust of bread, and if you please, add an ounce of pearl barley, or rice. Cover all close, and stew it till tender. Then take out the herbs, spices, and bread, and add a French

Vegetables

To dress Cauliflowers.

TAKE your flowers, cut off all the green pa
and then cut the flowers into four, and lay the
into water for an hour : then have some milk a
water boiling, put in the cauliflowers, and be su
to skim the sauce-pan well.   When the stalks a
tender, take them carefully up, and put them in
a cullender to drain : then put a spoonful of wat
into a clean stew-pan with a little dust of flou
about a quarter of a pound of butter, and sha
it round till it is all finely melted, with a lit
pepper and salt ; then take half the cauliflower a
cut it as you would for pickling, lay it into t
stew-pan, turn it, and shake the pan round.   T
minutes will do it.   Lay the stewed in the mid
of your plate, and the boiled round it.   Pour t
butter you did it in over it, and send it to table.

Another way.

CUT the cauliflower stalks off, leave a lit
green on and boil them in spring water and sa
about fifteen minutes will do them.   Take the
out and drain them ; send them whole in a di
with some melted butter in a cup.

To dress French Beans.

FIRST string them, and cut them in two, a
afterwards across ; but if you would do the
nice, cut the bean into four, and then across, whi
is eight pieces.   Lay them into water and s
and when your pan boils put in some salt and t
beans, when they are tender they are enoug
they will be soon done.   Take care they do
lose their fine green.   Lay them in a plate a
have butter in a cup.

To dress Artichokes.

WRING off the stalks, and put them into c

Cauliflower Florets
Two Ways

Adapted from "To dress Cauliflowers," Hannah Glasse, *The Art of Cookery Made Plain and Easy.*

Serves 4 to 6

This presentation of boiled and fried florets turns cauliflower into party food. With only salt and pepper as flavoring, the flavor of the vegetable is either pristine or plain, depending on your view of the merits of cauliflower.

INGREDIENTS
1 head of cauliflower
2 tablespoons unsalted butter
1 tablespoon olive oil
½ tablespoon all-purpose flour

1. Core the cauliflower by cutting out the thick stem on the underside and removing it as a wedge.
2. Cut the head into large florets, about 1½ to 3 inches.
3. Put the florets into a pot of boiling water, bring the water back to a boil, and boil just for a few minutes until you can pierce the floret stems with a fork.
4. Immediately drain the florets using a colander and cut half of them into smaller pieces.
5. In a heavy, medium-sized pan on medium heat, melt the butter and heat the oil with 1 tablespoon of water. Once the butter is completely melted, add the flour and stir gently. The mixture will bubble. Add the smaller florets and cook over medium heat for 7 to 10 minutes, turning occasionally, until all of the florets are coated with the butter/oil mixture and browning nicely.
6. Serve on a platter with the browned florets in the middle, surrounded by the larger boiled florets.

Dutch-Style Red Cabbage

Adapted from "Red cabbage dressed after the Dutch way, good for a cold in the breast," Hannah Glasse, *The Art of Cookery Made Plain and Easy*.

Serves 6 to 8

This ever-so-slightly tart red cabbage goes well with a hearty plain beef or chicken main course. It keeps well refrigerated and can be eaten cold as a side dish (reminiscent of sauerkraut) with sandwiches. To provide a more complex flavor, add a peeled and finely chopped apple during the cooking.

INGREDIENTS

1 small-medium head of cabbage (2 to 3 pounds), hard outer leaves removed, cored, and cut into shreds

2 tablespoons oil

2 tablespoons unsalted butter

2 tablespoons cider or sherry vinegar, plus an extra splash (to reduce the cabbage odor as it cooks)

1 onion, peeled and finely diced

¼ teaspoon or more kosher or sea salt

Freshly ground black pepper

1. Put the cabbage into a pot and cover with boiling water and a splash of the vinegar. Cook the cabbage for 5 minutes, then drain using a colander and run cold water over the cabbage, pressing out any excess water.

2. Heat the oil, butter, and vinegar in the pot, along with the onion, salt, pepper, and ¾ cup water.

3. Return the cabbage to the pot, stirring the onion and liquid into the cabbage. Simmer the mixture on low heat until the liquid has almost completely evaporated.

piece of white paper, oil it, and lay under the pasty, and bake it; it is best cold, and will keep a month.

Mackrel done the same way; head and tail together folded in a pasty, eats fine.

Asparagus dressed the Spanish way.

TAKE the asparagus, break them in pieces, then boil them soft, and drain the water from them: take a little oil, water and vinegar, let it boil, season it with pepper and salt, throw in the asparagus, and thicken with yolks of eggs.

Endive done this way, is good; the Spaniards add sugar, but that spoils them. Green pease done as above, are very good; only add a lettuce cut small, and two or three onions, and leave out the eggs.

Red cabbage dressed after the Dutch way, good for a cold in the breast.

TAKE the cabbage, cut it small, and boil it soft, then drain it, and put it in a stew-pan, with a sufficient quantity of oil and butter, a little water and vinegar, and an onion cut small; season it with pepper and salt, and let it simmer on a slow fire, till all the liquor is wasted.

Cauliflowers dressed the Spanish way.

BOIL them, but not too much; then drain them, and put them into a stew-pan; to a large cauliflower put a quarter of a pint of sweet oil, and two or three cloves of garlick; let them fry till brown; then season them with pepper and salt, two or three spoonfuls of vinegar; cover the pan very close, and let them simmer over a very slow fire an hour.

Carrots and French beans dressed the Dutch way.

SLICE the carrots very thin, and just cover them with water; season them with pepper and salt, cut a good many onions and parsley small, a piece of butter; let them simmer over a slow fire till done. Do French beans the same way.

Beans dressed the German way.

TAKE a large bunch of onions, peel and slice them, a great quantity of parsley washed and cut small, throw them into a stew-pan, with a pound of butter; season them well with pepper

and

Salad

Salamagundy Salad

Adapted from "To make Salamagundy," Hannah Glasse, *The Art of Cookery Made Plain and Easy.*

Serves 4 to 6 as a lunch or a side at dinner

This recipe is a layered version of what we might call a chopped salad today. Each ingredient is in a separate layer, beginning with meat on the bottom and ending with salad greens on top. To serve, just dive in with serving implements and the salad mixes together on the plate or in the bowl. I used a large, straight-sided soufflé dish; it would also look lovely in a large glass bowl. The name "salamgundy" or "salamagundi" comes from the French word salmigondis, *meaning a disparate collection of people or things. In old French cooking, a salmigondis was a mélange of different meats, reheated together in a sauce.*

SALAD INGREDIENTS

1 roasted chicken, cut or shredded into bite-sized
   pieces
6 hard-boiled eggs, whites and yolks minced separately
2 to 4 ounces (1 to 2 small tins) anchovies, minced
4 to 6 lemons, juiced and pulp removed and chopped
   (reserve the juice for dressing)
⅔ cup (about 4 to 6 ounces) minced sweet pickle chips
3 to 6 ounces sorrel, kale, or arugula, chopped or sliced
   into ribbons
6 ounces spinach, preferably baby spinach, chopped

SALAD DRESSING

6 ounces lemon juice (reserved juice from lemons
   used in salad)
6 ounces extra-virgin olive oil
1 teaspoon Dijon mustard
½ teaspoon kosher or coarse sea salt
Freshly ground black pepper

To Make the Salad

1. Place the pieces of chicken in a layer at the bottom of a large bowl or dish.
2. Add the rest of the ingredients in the order listed (minced egg yolks, then the egg whites, anchovies, lemon pulp, pickles, and greens). If using kale, gently massage the leaves and cut off the thick ribs before rolling the leaves and chopping or slicing them. If the spinach has heavy stems, remove those before chopping the spinach leaves.

To Make the Dressing

1. Whisk the ingredients together or shake them in a covered jar until the mixture has emulsified (the oil is suspended in the lemon juice and the mixture is a uniform yellow color).
2. Pour about half of the dressing over the top of the salad just before serving and serve the rest in a small pitcher for those who want extra.

thoroughly hot, pour it into your dish. Hash beef the same way.

To make Collops of cold Beef.

If you have any cold inside of a sirloin of beef, take off all the fat, cut it very thin in little bits, cut an onion very small, boil as much water or gravy as you think will do for sauce ; season it with a little pepper and salt, and a bundle of sweet herbs. Let the water boil, then put in the meat, with a good piece of butter rolled in flour, shake it round, and stir it. When the sauce is thick, and the meat done, take out the sweet herbs, and pour it into your dish. They do better than fresh meat

To make Salmagundy.

Mince two chickens, either boiled or roasted, very fine, or veal, if you please : also mince the yolks of hard eggs very small, and mince the whites very small by themselves ; shred the pulp of two or three lemons very small, then lay in your dish a layer of mince-meat, and a layer of yolks of eggs, a layer of whites, a layer of anchovies, a layer of your shred lemon pulp, a layer of pick-les, a layer of sorrel, a layer of spinach, and sha-lots shred small. When you have filled a dish with the ingredients, set an orange or lemon on the top ; then garnish with horse-radish scraped, barberries, and sliced lemon. Beat up some oil with the juice of lemon, salt, and mustard, thick, and serve it up for a second course, side dish, or middle-dish, for supper.

To make Essence of Ham.

Take a ham, and cut off all the fat, cut the lean in thin pieces, and lay them in the bottom of your stew-pan : put over them six onions sliced, two carrots, and one parsnip, two or three leeks, a

Sweets

Apple Pie

Adapted from "To Make an Apple Pye," Hannah Glasse, *The Art of Cookery Made Plain and Easy.*

Serves 8 to 10 (one large, deep dish 9-inch pie)

This pie should be served warm, in order to make its crust flaky. If serving after it cools, re-warm the pie at 325°F until the crust is warm to the touch. A mix of tart and sweet apples works nicely, e.g., Granny Smith, Red or Yellow Delicious, and Honeycrisp.

INGREDIENTS

1 recipe of puff pastry (see page 112), store-bought puff pastry, or another pie dough recipe, enough for 2 crusts

4 pounds apples (about 6 large) of various types that hold their shape when cooked, cored, peeled, and quartered, reserving the peels and cores

1 lemon, rind grated and then squeezed to yield 2 teaspoons juice

¾ cup granulated sugar, plus more to taste

¼ teaspoon ground mace

½ teaspoon ground cloves

2 tablespoons cornstarch

OPTIONAL

2 to 3 tablespoons milk

1½ teaspoons to 1 tablespoon demerara sugar

1. Divide the pastry dough in half. Place half back in the refrigerator. Roll out (or unwrap if store-bought) the second half and place into a 9-inch deep dish pie pan. Cover the pastry with plastic wrap and refrigerate while preparing the apples.

2. Cut each apple quarter into slices and put the apple slices into a bowl with the lemon rind, lemon juice, mace, cloves, sugar, and cornstarch. Mix until combined, and set aside.

3. Put the apple peels, cores, and 1 to 1¼ cups water in a small pot. Boil the mixture until the water reduces to slightly more than ¼ cup. Remove from the heat.

4. Take the pie plate lined with crust out of the refrigerator. Add the sliced apple mixture, and pour the slightly thickened liquid from the boiled peels and cores over the pie.

5. Refrigerate the filled pie while preheating the oven to 425°F.

6. Once the oven is preheated, roll out (or unwrap) the reserved half of the pastry. Take the filled pie out of the refrigerator, place the rolled-out pastry on top, and crimp the bottom and top crusts together. If desired, brush the top with milk and dust with sugar. Use a sharp knife to cut about six vents in the top crust.

7. Place the pie on a baking sheet (to catch any drips) and bake 15 minutes. Lower the temperature to 375°F and continue baking about 50 to 60 minutes more, until the top is nicely browned and the apple juices are bubbling. If the top browns too quickly, loosely place a piece of foil on top of the pie until the pie is done baking.

8. Let the warm pie cool before slicing.

may put in fome hard Yolks of Eggs; if you cannot get
m, put in Milk; but Cream is beft. About two Pounds of
Root will do.

To make an Apple Pye.

AKE a good Puff-pafte Cruft, lay fome round the Sides of
the Difh, pare and quarter your Apples, and take out the
s, lay a Row of Apples thick, throw in Half your Sugar you
n for your Pye, mince a little Lemon-peel fine, throw over
fqueeze a little Lemon over them, then a few Cloves, here
there one, then the reft of your Apples, and the reft of your
r. You muft fweeten to your Palate, and fqueeze a little
e Lemon; boil the Peeling of the Apples, and the Cores in
fair Water, with a Blade of Mace, till it is very good;
n it and boil the Syrup with a little Sugar, till there is but
little and good, pour it into your Pye, put on your Upper-
, and bake it. You may put in a little Quince and Marma-
if you pleafe.

hus make a Pear Pye; but don't put in any Quince. You
butter them when they come out of the Oven; or beat up the
s of two Eggs, and Half a Pint of Cream, with a little Nut-
, fweetned with Sugar, take off the Lid, and pour in the
m. Cut the Cruft in little three corner Pieces, and ftick about
Pye, and fend it to Table.

To make a Cherry Pye.

AKE a good Cruft, lay a little round the Sides of your Difh,
throw Sugar at the Bottom, and lay in your Fruit and Sugar
op. A few red Currants does well with them; put on your
and bake in a flack Oven.

ake a Plumb Pye the fame Way, and a Goofeberry Pye. If
would have it red, let it ftand a good while in the Oven, af-
he Bread is drawn. A Cuftard is very good with the Goofe-
Pye.

To make a Salt-Fifh Pye.

ET a Side of Salt-Fifh, lay it in Water all Night, next Morning put it over the Fire in a Pan of Water till it is tender,
it, and lay it on the Dreffer, take off all the Skin, and pick
Meat clean from the Bones, mince it fmall, then take the
nb of two *French* Rolls, cut in Slices, and boiled up with a
t of new Milk, break your Bread very fine with a Spoon, put
your minced Salt-Fifh, a Pound of melted Butter, two Spoonfuls

Chocolate Puffs

Adapted from "Chocolate Puffs," Richard Briggs,
The New Art of Cookery.

Makes about 2 dozen

These tiny sweets are a cross between cookies and candy. They are crisp, intensely chocolatey, and addictive.

INGREDIENTS

1 cup plus 2 tablespoons superfine sugar
¼ cup plus 1¼ tablespoons unsweetened cocoa, preferably Dutch processed
1 egg white
pinch of cream of tartar, optional

1. Preheat the oven to 225°F. Set aside two parchment-lined cookie sheets.
2. In a medium-small bowl, whisk together the sugar and cocoa until they are a uniform color. Set the mixture aside.
3. With a hand beater, stand mixer, or clean whisk, whip the egg white until it is very frothy and beginning to stiffen. (When using a hand or stand mixer to whip egg whites, start at a low speed and slowly raise the speed to medium. Do not use the higher speeds because egg whites whipped that way are less stable.) If desired, add a pinch of cream of tartar to help the egg white froth and stiffen. Once the egg white reaches the soft peak stage, slowly add the sugar/cocoa mixture while continuing to beat the egg white. The result should be a thick paste.
4. Wet your hands slightly and form the batter into small coins about ¾-inch diameter. Place them on the parchment-lined cookie sheets and bake 1¼ to 1½ hours.
5. Store the cookies in a tightly covered container.

Chocolate Puffs.

TAKE half a pound of double-refined sugar, beat and sift it fine, scrape into it one ounce of chocolate very fine, and mix them together; beat up the white of an egg to a very high froth, then put in your chocolate and sugar, and beat it till it is as stiff as a paste; then strew sugar on some writing-paper, drop them on about the size of a sixpence, and bake them in a very low oven; when they are done take them off the paper and put them in plates.

Almond Puffs.

BLANCH and skin two ounces of almonds, and beat them fine in a mortar with orange-flower water; take the whites of three eggs, and beat them to a high froth, then put in some powder sugar finely sifted, mix your almonds with the sugar and eggs, and then add more sugar till it is as thick as a paste; strew some sugar on a sheet of writing-paper, lay it on in small cakes, and bake it in a cool oven.

Lemon Puffs.

BEAT a pound of double-refined sugar, sift it through a fine sieve, put it into a bowl, with the juice of two lemons strained through a sieve, and beat them well together; then beat up the white of an egg to a very high froth, put it into the lemon-juice and sugar, beat all well for half an hour, grate in the rind of two lemons, beat up three eggs and put in, and mix it well up; sprinkle some sugar on writing-paper, drop on the mixture in small drops, and bake them a few minutes in a moderate oven.

CHAP.

Hall, the magnificent ancestral estate of Mrs. Levering's family in England.

SOFT GINGER BREAD

(*Glen Ellen*)

Two pounds flour, 1 pound butter, 1 pound brown sugar, 1 pint molasses, 6 eggs. Cream, butter and sugar together, then add flour and molasses alternately; half of the flour retained and beaten in alternately with the eggs. Grated lemon peel, allspice, cinnamon and ginger; 2 teaspoonfuls of soda in molasses.

Mrs. Robert Gilmor,
Glen Ellen.

BLACKBERRY PUDDING (EXCELLENT)

(*Glen Ellen*)

Four tablespoonfuls of flour, $\frac{1}{2}$ pint of milk, yolks of 4 eggs, $\frac{1}{4}$ pound of butter, $\frac{3}{4}$ pound brown sugar, nutmeg to taste, wine if you choose. Mix as a batter; add 1 pint of blackberries mixed in gradually. Bake in a greased dish faster than cake. Serve with " Nuns' Butter Sauce." Mrs. Robert Gilmor.

Gingerbread Cake

Adapted from "Soft Ginger Bread," Mrs. Robert Gilmor's recipe, Maude A. Bomberger, *Colonial Recipes*.

Serves 8 to 10 (one 9-inch round cake, about 2-inches tall)

This moist, rich cake is flavorful without being overwhelming. For an easy decorative finish, dust the top with confectioners sugar. Alternatively, mix 1 to 2 cups of confectioners sugar with a few drops of lemon juice, water, or milk to and drizzle that glaze over the top, letting it run down the sides of the cake. This recipe proportion is cut in half from the original, which would have made an enormous cake.

INGREDIENTS

3 cups all-purpose flour
2 teaspoons ground ginger
½ teaspoon ground cinnamon
¼ teaspoon ground allspice
1 teaspoon baking soda
16 tablespoons (8 ounces or 2 sticks) unsalted butter, at room temperature
¾ cup packed light brown sugar
½ cup granulated sugar
boiling water
1 cup unsulphured molasses
Zest from ½ lemon (about 1 teaspoon zest)
2 large eggs at room temperature, lightly beaten

1. Preheat the oven to 350°F. Spray or butter a 9-inch round pan with 2-inch sides. Put parchment or foil on the bottom and spray again, then put a ring of foil around the sides of the pan and spray or butter the foil.

2. Whisk together the flour, ginger, cinnamon, allspice, and baking soda in a bowl. Set aside.

3. Cream the butter and the sugars. If using a stand or hand mixer, use medium speed for at least 3 minutes until the butter and sugars are completely combined and whipped until light and airy.

4. Add ½ cup boiling water to the molasses and stir the mixture until completely combined. Add the lemon zest.

5. The creamed butter and sugars will be the "base" of the batter. The dry mixture (flour/spices/baking soda), the molasses/water mixture, and the eggs are added as follows: add approximately half of the flour mixture in three portions to the creamed butter and sugars, alternately with the molasses in two portions, beginning and ending with the flour mixture. (No need to be precise in measuring.) Once that mixture is well combined, add the second half of the flour mixture with the eggs, with the flour mixture in three portions and the eggs in two. Mix gently until well combined.

6. Spoon the stiff batter into the prepared cake pan. Using a knife or spatula, smooth the batter out, and bake for 45 to 60 minutes, until a cake tester inserted in the middle comes out clean. Let the cake rest in its pan for 10 minutes, then invert it onto a wire rack and cool completely.

7. Well wrapped, this cake will stay moist at room temperature for several days.

Vanilla Ice Cream

Adapted from Thomas Jefferson's handwritten notes.

Makes 1 quart

This version makes half as much as Jefferson's recipe and requires an ice cream maker. I added vanilla and a bit of salt, which are not part of Jefferson's recipe, but the proportions of cream, egg yolks, and sugar are those he prescribed. I generally used the method recommended by one of my favorite food websites, Serious Eats, *to create the custard. The result is rich and creamy.*

INGREDIENTS
3 large eggs, yolks only
   (reserve whites for another dish)
¾ cup granulated sugar
1 quart (4 cups) heavy cream
1½ to 2 teaspoons vanilla extract
½ teaspoon kosher or sea salt

1. In a medium-sized heavy pot, whisk the egg yolks and sugar together about 2 minutes, until they form a thickened, light-colored mixture that makes a ribbon when you lift the whisk. Be sure to gather all of the ingredients from the edges of the pot as you whisk.

2. Slowly pour in the cream, whisking as you add it, until the egg yolks, sugar, and cream are well combined.

3. Using a wooden spoon, heat the mixture over medium-low heat, stirring frequently in a circular motion that scrapes the bottom of the pot and around the sides. Cook the mixture to turn it into a custard. To test whether it is at that custard stage, use a thermometer; at custard stage, the mixture will be around 170°F, which is hot but well below a simmer. Or, coat the wooden spoon and run your finger across the back; if your finger leaves a clean line, the mixture is ready. This process may take as long as 20 to 30 minutes. It's better to keep the heat on the low side and take longer than to scorch the bottom of the pot or overcook the mixture.

4. Take the pot off the heat, add the vanilla extract and salt, and stir to combine. Then strain the custard into a heatproof bowl and refrigerate it at least until it is well chilled, preferably overnight.

5. Once the mixture is completely chilled, follow manufacturer's directions for the ice cream maker, churning the ice cream until it looks close to the consistency of soft serve. A spoon or spatula gently scraped along the top should leave a well-defined ridge.

6. Chill the ice cream in a plastic container until its consistency is "scoopable."

Ice cream.

2 bottles of good cream.

6. yolks of eggs.

½ lb sugar

mix the yolks & sugar

put the cream on a fire in a casse
-role, first putting in a stick of vanilla.

when near boiling take it off &
pour it gently into the mixture
of eggs & sugar.

stir it well.

put it on the fire again stirring
it thoroughly with a spoon to
prevent it's sticking to the casse
-role.

when near boiling take it off and
strain it thro' a towel.

put it in the Sabotiere.

then set it in ice an hour before
it is to be served. put into the
ice a handful of salt.

put ice all round the Sabotiere
i.e. a layer of ice a layer of salt
for three layers.

put salt on the coverlid of the
Sabotiere & cover the whole with
ice.

leave it still half a quarter of an
hour.

then turn the Sabotiere in the
ice 10 minutes

open it to loosen with a spatule
the ice from the inner sides of
the Sabotiere.

shut it & replace it in the ice.

open it from time to time to de-
-tach the ice from the sides

when well taken (prise) stir it
well with the Spatule.

put it in moulds, justling it
well down on the knee.

then put the mould into the
same bucket of ice.

leave it there to the moment
of serving it.

to withdraw it, immerse the
mould in warm water,
turning it well till it
will come out & turn it
into a plate.

Puff Pastry

Adapted from "Puff Paste," Hannah Glasse, *The Art of Cookery Made Plain and Easy*.

Makes enough for 1 double-crust deep dish pie and 1 open-faced pie, plus a bit extra

This adaptation halves Hannah Glasse's recipe and updates the ingredient references, but generally follows her technique. She used puff pastry in pies (including the apple pie in this book) where we modern cooks would probably use simpler pie dough recipes. Served warm, this crust is simply heavenly; buttery and flaky as you cut through to the pie filling.

INGREDIENTS

3⅓ cups all-purpose flour, plus more to flour the surface of your work area

¼ teaspoon salt, preferably fine sea salt

24 tablespoons (¾ pound or 3 sticks) unsalted butter, well chilled

1. Whisk the salt into the flour. Then cut 8 tablespoons (¼ pound or 1 stick) butter into small pieces and mix it into the flour by hand, with a pastry cutter or knives, or with a food processor. Do not overmix.

2. Add ½ cup or more of ice water by tablespoons or in a thin stream, combining it with the flour and butter, just until the dough begins to hold together.

3. Dump the dough onto a silicone mat or other pastry-friendly surface and form it into a ball. Cover the ball in plastic wrap; refrigerate it for 1 hour.

4. After the dough has chilled, roll it into a rectangle on a lightly floured surface, add dots of slightly chilled butter on top, and fold it into thirds. Repeat the process 9 or 10 times using up the remaining 16 tablespoons (½ pound or 2 sticks) of butter as dots on top of the dough in the process.

5. The dough is now ready to be rolled out for the apple or other pie. Freeze any remaining dough tightly wrapped in plastic.

Puff-Paste.

TAKE a Quarter of a Peck of Flour, rub fine Half a Pound of Butter, a little Salt, make it up into a light Paste with cold Water, just stiff enough to work it well up; then roll it out, and stick Pieces of Butter all over, and strew a little Flour; roll it up, and roll it out again; and so do nine or ten Times, till you have rolled in a Pound and Half of Butter. This Crust is mostly used for all Sorts of Pies.

A good Crust for Great Pies.

TO a Peck of Flour the Yolk of three Eggs, then boil some Water, and put in Half a Pound of try'd Sewet, and a Pound and Half of Butter. Skim off the Butter and Sewet, and as much of the Liquor as will make it a light good Crust; work it up well, and roll it out.

A Standing Crust for Great Pies.

TAKE a Peck of Flour, and six Pounds of Butter, boiled in a Gallon of Water, skim it off into the Flour, and as little of the Liquor as you can; work it well up into a Paste, then pull it into Pieces till it is cold, then make it up in what Form you will have it. This is fit for the Walls of a Goose Pye.

A Cold Crust.

TO three Pounds of Flour, rub in a Pound and Half of Butter; break in two Eggs, and make it up with cold Water.

A Dripping Crust.

TAKE a Pound and Half of Beef-dripping, boil it in Water, strain it, then let it stand to be cold, and take off the hard Fat; scrape it, boil it so four or five Times; then work it well up into three Pounds of Flour, as fine as you can, and make it up into Paste with cold Water, it makes a very fine Crust.

A Crust for Custards.

TAKE Half a Pound of Flour, six Ounces of Butter, the Yolks of two Eggs, three Spoonfuls of Cream, mix them together, and let them stand a Quarter of an Hour, then work it up and down, and roll it very thin.

Paste

Beverages

Hot Chocolate

Adapted from "To make Chocolate," Elizabeth Raffald, *The Experienced English House-Keeper.*

Serves 1

This dairy-free hot chocolate is rich and quite satisfying. To scale it up for multiple servings, simply use a larger pot and increase the water and cocoa in proportion.

INGREDIENTS

1 tablespoon unsweetened cocoa,
    preferably Dutch processed
2 tablespoons sugar

1. Put the cocoa in a small pot.
2. Pour ¾ cup boiling water over the cocoa and whisk the mixture until the cocoa is completely dissolved. Add the sugar and bring the mixture to a boil. Whisk it again and let the mixture sit at least 1 to 2 hours or overnight.
3. After the resting period, whisk the mixture, bring it back to a boil and boil for 2 minutes, then whisk it again until foam develops on the top.
4. Serve immediately.

N. B. You may leave out the Wine and Sugar, and put in a little good Cream and a little Salt, if you like it better.

To make Chocolate.

SCRAPE four Ounces of Chocolate and pour a Quart of boiling Water upon it, mill it well with a Chocolate Mill, and fweeten it to your Tafte, give it a boil and let it ftand all Night, then mill it again very well, boil it two Minutes, then mill it 'till it will leave a Froth upon the Top of your Cups.

***

CHAP. XV.

Obfervations on Wines, Catchup, and Vinegar.

WINE is a very neceffary Thing in moft Families, and is often fpoiled through Mifmanagement of putting together, for if you let it ftand too long before you get it cold, and don't take great Care to put your Barm upon it in Time, it Summer-beams and blinks in the Tub, fo that it makes your Wine fret in the Cafk, and will not let it fine; it is equally as great a Fault to let it work too long in the Tub, for that takes off all the Sweetnefs and Flavour of the Fruit or Flowers your Wine is made from, fo the only Caution I can give, is to be careful in following the Receipts, and to have your Veffels dry, rinfe them with

Brandy,

sweeten it to your Taste, then put in the Juice of a Lemon, and a Glass of Madeira Wine, or French Brandy, mill it to a Froth with a Chocolate Mill, and take it off as it rises, and lay it upon a Hair Sieve, then fill one half of your Posset Glasses, a little more than half full with White Wine, and the other half of your Glasses a little more than half full of Red Wine, then lay on your Froth as high as you can, but observe that it is well drained on your Sieve, or it will mix with your Wine, and spoil your Syllabubs.

To make Lemon Syllabubs *a second Way*.

Put a Pint of Cream to a Pint of White Wine, then rub a quarter of a Pound of Loaf Sugar upon the out Rind of two Lemons, 'till you have got out all the Essence, then put the Sugar to the Cream, and squeeze in the Juice of both Lemons, let it stand for two Hours, then mill them with a Chocolate Mill, to raise the Froth, and take it off with a Spoon as it rises, or it will make it heavy, lay it upon a Hair Sieve to drain, then fill your Glasses with the Remainder, and lay on the Froth as high as you can, let them stand all Night, and they will be clear at the Bottom; send them to the Table upon a Salver, with Jellies.

To make a Syllabub *under the* Cow.

Put a Bottle of strong Beer, and a Pint of Cyder into a Punch Bowl, grate in a small Nutmeg,

Lemon Syllabub

Adapted from "To make Lemon Syllabubs a Second Way," Elizabeth Raffald, *The Experienced English House-Keeper.*

Serves 2

This simple whipped syllabub is an elegant drink/dessert. Its creamy froth rises to the top of a glass, leaving a refreshing lemony wine on the bottom. Although it takes only minutes to prepare, allow several hours between preparation and serving so that the froth and liquid have time to separate. Use glasses wide enough to allow a spoon for eating the topping, which is similar to a lemon mousse. Select a white wine variety based on how sweet you want the syllabub to be. (Keep in mind that the topping resembles lemon mousse.) Using a dry white such as a Sauvignon Blanc or Pinot Grigio will make the syllabub a bit tart, while a sweeter white, such as a Chenin Blanc or a Reisling, will make the syllabub taste more like a sweet dessert.

INGREDIENTS

1 lemon, cut in half, with rind grated from half and juice from one or both halves for a total of ¼ cup juice
½ cup granulated sugar
1 cup white wine
1 cup heavy cream

1. Rub the grated lemon rind into the sugar with your fingers until they are well combined. Mix the rind, sugar, lemon juice, and the wine.
2. Add the cream and whisk the mixture until it froths. Gently pour it into two glasses. Let them stand on a counter for about 2 hours, then refrigerate until serving. As the glasses sit, the froth will rise, leaving the lemony wine on the bottom of the glasses.

Fresh Strawberry Water

Adapted from "Fresh Strawberry Water," Frederic Nutt, *The Complete Confectioner.*

Serves 2 to 3

This refreshing fruit water is easily made with a blender and a colander or strainer. The same technique can be used for a variety of berry fruit waters. The measurement of strawberries contained in the original recipe, "one pottle," is not exact. Pottles were conical baskets in which strawberries were sold. At one point a pottle was the equivalent of a quart (roughly 1½ pounds), but later it was half that (a pint.) I used a measurement in-between. Keep in mind that the amount of sugar may have to be adjusted depending on the sweetness of your berries.

INGREDIENTS

16 ounces fresh strawberries, hulled and coarsely chopped
2 tablespoons confectioners (powdered) sugar
Juice of 1 lemon (about ¼ cup)
Garnishes such as a lemon slice or a reserved strawberry, optional

1. Mash the strawberries into a pulp using a blender or potato masher. Strain the juice into a bowl or measuring cup by pressing the pulp through a strainer or colander.
2. Mix the confectioners sugar and lemon juice into the strawberry juice.
3. Fill 1 large glass or 2 to 3 smaller ones with ice, add the juice, and top with a few splashes of water. (Use no more than ½ to ¾ cup of water for the 1 to 3 glasses.) Garnish, if desired, with lemon slices or strawberries.

to make it palatable; pass it through a
lawn sieve and it is fit for use.

No. 118. *Fresh Strawberry Water.*

TAKE one pottle of strawberries and
pick the stalks from them; pass them
through a sieve with your wooden spoon;
and put in two large spoonfuls of powdered sugar; squeeze one lemon, and let
the rest be water; make it palatable, pass
it through a sieve and it is fit for use.

No. 119. *Barberry Water.*

TAKE two large spoonfuls of bar-
berry jam and put them in a bason;
squeeze two lemons, put in one gill of
syrup and the rest water; put a little
cochineal in, and if you find it not rich
enough put a little more syrup, make
it

Measurement Conversions

VOLUME EQUIVALENTS (LIQUID)

US STANDARD	US STANDARD (OUNCES)	METRIC (APPROX)
2 tablespoons	1 fl. oz.	30 mL
¼ cup	2 fl. oz.	60 mL
½ cup	4 fl. oz.	120 mL
1 cup	8 fl. oz.	240 mL
1½ cups	12 fl. oz.	355 mL
2 cups or 1 pint	16 fl. oz.	475 mL
4 cups or 1 quart	32 fl. oz.	1 L
1 gallon	128 fl. oz.	4 L

OVEN TEMPERATURES

FAHRENHEIT (F)	CELSIUS (C) (APPROXIMATE)
250°F	120°C
300°F	150°C
325°F	165°C
350°F	180°C
375°F	190°C
400°F	200°C
425°F	220°C
450°F	230°C

VOLUME EQUIVALENTS (DRY)

US STANDARD	METRIC (APPROX)
⅛ teaspoon	0.5 mL
¼ teaspoon	1 mL
½ teaspoon	2 mL
¾ teaspoon	4 mL
1 teaspoon	5 mL
1 tablespoon	15 mL
¼ cup	59 mL
⅓ cup	79 mL
½ cup	118 mL
⅔ cup	156 mL
¾ cup	177 mL
1 cup	235 mL
2 cups or 1 pint	475 mL
3 cups	700 mL
4 cups or 1 quart	1 L

WEIGHT EQUIVALENTS

US STANDARD	METRIC (APPROX)
½ ounce	15 g
1 ounce	30 g
2 ounces	60 g
4 ounces	115 g
8 ounces	225 g
12 ounces	340 g
16 oz or 1 lb	455 g

STANDARD CUP EQUIVALENTS

STANDARD CUP	FLOURS	GRAINS	GRANULARS	LIQUID SOLIDS	LIQUIDS
1 cup	140g	150g	190g	200g	240ml
¾ cup	105g	113g	143g	150g	180ml
⅔ cup	93g	100g	125g	133g	160ml
½ cup	70g	75g	95g	100g	120ml
⅓ cup	47g	50g	63g	67g	80ml
¼ cup	35g	38g	48g	50g	60ml
⅛ cup	18g	19g	24g	25g	30ml

Bibliography of Original Recipes

The recipes are listed in the order they appear, with the name of the original recipe in quotes and the name of the adapted recipe in *italics*. The citation is to the book (including edition and page), or in the case of the ice cream recipe, the webpage, where the original recipe appears.

Breakfast & Breads

Bread Pudding

Original title: "A Bread Pudding"

Adaptation: *Bread Pudding*

Amelia Simmons, *American Cookery*, or the art of dressing viands, fish, poultry, and vegetables: and the best modes of making pastes, puffs, pies, tarts, puddings, custards, and preserves: and all kinds of cakes, from the imperial plumb to plain cake, adapted to this country and all grades of life. (Hartford: Hudson & Goodwin for the Author, 1796), 26. Bitting Collection, Rare Book and Special Collections Division of the Library of Congress, Washington, DC.

English Rabbit

Original title: "To make an English Rabbit"

Adaptation: *Toaster Oven English Rabbit*

Hannah Glasse, *The Art of Cookery, Made Plain and Easy; Which far exceed any Thing of the Kind ever yet published.* (London: The author, first published pseudonymously ("By a lady"), 1747), 190. Bitting Collection, Rare Book and Special Collections Division of the Library of Congress, Washington, DC.

Johnny or Hoe Cakes

Original title: "Johny Cake, or Hoe Cake"

Adaptation: Johnny or Hoe Cakes

Simmons, *American Cookery*, 34.

Soups

Split Pea Soup

Original title: "Another Green Peas Soup"

Adaptation: *Split Pea Soup*

Richard Briggs, *The English Art of Cookery*, According to the Present Practice: being a Complete Guide to all Housekeepers on a Plan Entirely New, Consisting of Thirty-eight Chapters. (London: Printed for G.G. and J. Robinson, 1794), 28. Elizabeth Robins Pennell Collection, Rare Book and Special Collections Division of the Library of Congress, Washington, DC.

West Indian Pepper Pot Soup

Original title: "A West-India Pepper Pot"

Adaptation: *West Indian Pepper Pot Soup*

Briggs, *The English Art of Cookery*, 34–35.

Fish & Seafood

Baked Whole Whitefish

Original title: "To bake a Turbot"

Adaptation: *Baked Whole Whitefish*

Hannah Glasse, *The Art of Cookery, Made Plain and Easy; Which far exceed any Thing of the Kind ever yet published.* (Fredricksburg, Printed by Cottom and Stewart, 1805), 47. Bitting Collection, Rare Book and Special Collections Division of the Library of Congress, Washington, DC.

Scalloped Oysters

Original title: "To make Scollops of Oysters"

Adaptation: *Scalloped Oysters*

Glasse, *The Art of Cookery*, 1805 ed., 56.

Meats

Beef à la Mode

Original title: "Beef à la Mode in Pieces"

Adaptation: *Beef à la Mode*

Glasse, *The Art of Cookery*, 1747 ed., 36.

Fried Sausages and Apples

Original title: "Fried Sausages"

Adaptation: *Fried Sausages and Apples*

Glasse, *The Art of Cookery*, 1805 ed., 90.

Lamb Stew

Original title: "A Harrico of Mutton"

Adaptation: *Lamb Stew*

Glasse, *The Art of Cookery*, 1747 ed., 45.

Slow Cooker Corned Beef

Original title: "To Stew Brisket of Beef"

Adaptation: *Slow Cooker Corned Beef*

Richard Briggs, *The New Art of Cookery*, According to the Present Practice: being a Complete Guide to all Housekeepers on a Plan Entirely New, Consisting of Thirty-eight Chapters. (Philadelphia: Printed for W. Spotswood, R. Campbell, and E. Johnson. 1792), 81. Bitting Collection, Rare Book and Special Collections Division of the Library of Congress, Washington, DC.

Vegetables

Cauliflower Florets Two Ways

Original title: "To dress Cauliflowers"

Adaptation: *Cauliflower Florets Two Ways*

Glasse, *The Art of Cookery*, 1805 ed., 34.

Dutch-Style Red Cabbage

Original title: "Red cabbage dressed after the Dutch way, good for a cold in the breast"

Adaptation: *Dutch-Style Red Cabbage*

Hannah Glasse, *The Art of Cookery, Made Plain and Easy; Which far exceed any Thing of the Kind ever yet published.* (London: printed for A. Millar, J. and R. Tonson, W. Strahan, T. Caslon, Bl. Law and A. Hamilton, 1763), 343. Pennell Collection, Rare Book and Special Collections Division of the Library of Congress, Washington, DC.

Salad

Salamagundy Salad

Original title: "To make Salamagundy"

Adaptation: *Salamagundy Salad*

Glasse, *The Art of Cookery*, 1805 ed., 93.

Sweets

Apple Pie

Original title: "To make an Apple Pye"

Adaptation: *Apple Pie*

Glasse, *The Art of Cookery*, 1747 ed., 225.

Chocolate Puffs

Original title: "Chocolate Puffs"

Adaptation: *Chocolate Puffs*

Briggs, *The New Art of Cookery*, 367.

Gingerbread Cake

Original title: "Soft Ginger Bread"

Adaptation: Gingerbread Cake

Maude A. Bomberger, *Colonial Recipes from Old Virginia and Maryland Manors, with Numerous Legends and Traditions Interwoven* (New York and Washington: The Neale Publishing Company, 1907), 56. Bitting Collection, Rare Book and Special Collections Division of the Library of Congress, Washington, DC.

Vanilla Ice Cream

Original title: "Ice Cream"

Adaptation: Vanilla Ice Cream

Handwritten recipe in the holograph collection of the Library of Congress, Washington, DC. www.loc.gov/exhibits/treasures/images/uc004810.jpg. Accessed April 26, 2017. www.loc.gov/exhibits/treasures/tri034.html

Puff Pastry

Original title: "Puff Paste"

Adaptation: *Puff Pastry*

Glasse, *The Art of Cookery*, 1747 ed., 145.

Beverages

Hot Chocolate

Original title: "To make Chocolate"

Adaptation: *Hot Chocolate*

Elizabeth Raffald, *The Experienced English House-keeper*, for the Use and Ease of Ladies, House-keepers, Cooks & C. (Manchester, Printed by J. Haroup for the Author, 1769), page 295.

Lemon Syllabub

Original title: "To make Lemon Syllabubs a Second Way"

Adaptation: Lemon Syllabub

Raffald, *The Experienced English House-keeper,* page 184

Strawberry Water

Original title: "Fresh Strawberry Water"

Adaptation: Strawberry Water

Frederick Nutt, *The Complete Confectioner*; or The Whole Art of Confectionary; Forming a Ready Assistant to all Genteel Families; giving Them a Perfect Knowledge of Confectionary with Instructions, Neatly Engraved on Ten Copper-Plates, How to Decorate a Table with Taste and Elegance without the Expense or Assistance of a Confectioner. (London, Printed for the Author, 1790), 109. Bitting Collection, Rare Book and Special Collections Division of the Library of Congress, Washington, DC.

Endnotes

Introduction

1 Genevieve Foster, *George Washington's World* (New York: Scribner. 1941).

Chapter 1

2 For information on Hamilton's life, I consulted a number of sources. Ron Chernow's excellent and exhaustive biography, *Alexander Hamilton*, and Jeff Wilser's breezier and fun book, *Alexander Hamilton's Guide to Life* were both invaluable. In addition, if you are interested in the chronology of his life, see www.pbs.org/wgbh/amex/hamilton/timeline/timeline2.html.

3 There is disagreement about when Alexander Hamilton was born, 1755 or 1757. I have accepted the earlier date, the one adopted by Ron Chernow in his definitive biography, *Alexander Hamilton.*

4 Ankeet Ball, Ambition and Bondage: An Inquiry on Alexander Hamilton and Slavery, quoting from Syrett, Harold and Jacob E. Cooke, eds. *The Papers of Hamilton.* Vol 2. (New York: Columbia University Press, 1961-87), footnote 39, accessed April 17, 2017. columbiaandslavery.columbia.edu/content/ambition-bondage-inquiry-alexander-hamilton-and-slavery.

5 Hamilton to James McHenry, 7 January, 1799, in *The Hamilton Papers*, Founders Online, accessed April 18, 2017, founders.archives.gov/documents/Hamilton/01-22-02-0223.

Chapter 2

6 Kwasi, Konadu, "Slavery in the Danish Carribean," accessed April 17, 2017, www.afropedea.org/slavery-in-the-danish-caribbean.

7 William F. Cissel, "Alexander Hamilton: The West Indian 'Founding Father'," July 2004, 26 at footnote 44, accessed April 17, 2017, www.virginislandspace.org/Division%20of%20Libraries/cisselpaper.pdf.

8 James Oliver Horton, "Alexander Hamilton: Slavery and Race in a Revolutionary Generation," *New York Journal of American History*, Issue 3(Spring 2004), 17, accessed April 17, 2017, through www.alexanderhamiltonexhibition.org/about/teachers.html at www.alexanderhamiltonexhibition.org/about/Horton%20-%20Hamiltsvery_Race.pdf.

9 James T. Lemon, "Colonial Life in the Eighteenth Century," 121, accessed April 17, 2017. www.asdk12.org/staff/bivins_rick/HOMEWORK/230028_Colonial Life.pdf.

10 Ron Chernow, *Alexander Hamilton* (New York, The Penguin Press), page 147.

11 US Department of Commerce, Bureau of the Census, *Historical Statistics of the United States Colonial Times to 1970, Bicentennial Edition, volume 1* (Washington DC: Government Printing Office, 1975), 8, accessed April 17, 2017. fraser.stlouisfed.org/files/docs/publications/histstatus/hstat1970_cen_1975_v1.pdf

13 US Department of Commerce, Bureau of the Census, *Population in the Colonial and Continental Periods*, 11, accessed April 17, 2017, www2.census.gov/prod2/decennial/documents/00165897ch01.pdf.

14 US Department of Commerce, Bureau of the Census, *Urban, Urbanized Area, Urban Cluster, and Rural Population 2000 and 2010: United States*, accessed April 17, 2017, www.census.gov/geo/reference/ua/urban-rural-2010.html.

15 The Largest US Cities: Cities Ranked 1 to 100 and Cities Ranked 101 to 200, accessed April 17, 2017, www.citymayors.com/gratis/uscities_100.html.

16 Amy Chin, Brett Palfreyman, Valerie Paley. *Windows on the City, Looking out at Gracie's New York: A Curated Reinstallation of Gracie Mansion's Official Rooms on the*

35th Anniversary of the Gracie Mansion Conservancy (October 2015), 6, accessed April 17, 2017, www1.nyc. gov/assets/gracie/downloads/pdf/gmc_brochure.pdf.

17 Pauline Maier, *Boston and New York in the Eighteenth Century*, 182, Proceedings of the American Antiquarian Society, 91 (1981):177-195, 182, accessed April 17, 2017, www.americanantiquarian.org/ proceedings/44517672.pdf.

18 Chin, Palfreyman, and Paley, *Windows on the City*, 6, www1.nyc.gov/assets/gracie/downloads/pdf/gmc_ brochure.pdf.

19 New York Historical Society, History of Slavery in New York, accessed April 17, 2017, www.slaveryinnewyork. org/history.htm.

20 Maier, *Boston and New York*, 192, citing Charles Francis Adams, ed., *The Works of John Adams*, www. americanantiquarian.org/proceedings/44517672.pdf.

21 Frank Paul Mann, "The British Occupation of Southern New York during the American Revolution and the Failure to Restore Civilian Government" (PhD diss., Syracuse University, 2013), accessed April 17, 2017, surface.syr.edu/cgi/viewcontent.cgi?article =1099&context=hst_etd.

22 Edwin G. Burrows, "The Prisoners of New York" (paper presented at symposium, "The American Revolution on Long Island and in New York City," Stony Brook University, October 4, 2010, accessed on April 17, 2017, lihj.cc.stonybrook.edu/2012/articles/ the-prisoners-of-new-york/.

Chapter 3

23 Katherine Menz, "Historic Furnishings Report: Hamilton Grange National Monument," (1986), 7, *Hamilton Grange National Memorial*, accessed April 18, 2017, www.nps.gov/hagr/learn/historyculture/ upload/Historic-Furnishings-Report.pdf.

24 Danielle Funiciello, Schuyler Mansion Historic Site, e-mail message to author, February 3, 2017.

25 Nancy E. Richards, "The City Home of Benjamin Chew, Sr., and his Family: A Case Study of the Textures of Life," 13, accessed on April 17, 2017, www.cliveden.org/ wp-content/uploads/2013/09/Benjamin -Chew-townhouse.pdf.

26 Sandra L. Oliver, *Food in Colonial and Federal America* (Westport, Connecticut: Greenwood Press, 2005), pages 107–111.

27 *Early American Fireplaces and Cooking*, accessed April 17, 2017, colonial-american-life.blogspot. com/2009/08/early-american-fireplaces-and-cooking. html.

28 Sir Benjamin Thompson, Count von Rumford, accessed April 17, 2017, www.monticello.org/site/ research-and-collections/sir-benjamin-thompson -count-von-rumford#_ftnref5.

29 Alfred Mongin and Anne D. Whidden, "Historic Structure Report: Hamilton Grange National Memorial", (1980), 33, *Hamilton Grange National Memorial*, accessed April 18, 2017, www.nps.gov/ hagr/learn/historyculture/upload/Historic-Structure -Report.pdf.

30 Miller-Cory House Museum and the New Jersey Historical Society, Pleasures of Colonial Cooking, (New Jersey: New Jersey Historical Society, 1982), 6–7.

31 Early American Fireplaces and Cooking, accessed April 17, 2017, colonial-american-life.blogspot.com/ 2009/08/early-american-fireplaces-and-cooking.html.

32 Alexander Hamilton (Dr.), *Itinerarium*, (St. Louis, Missouri, printed privately, 1774) 99, accessed April 17, 2017, cdn.loc.gov/service/gdc/lhbtn/02374/ 02374.pdf.

33 Bill Bryson, "Every Fish Knife Tells a Story: Bill Bryson Reveals How the History in Our Homes has Changed the Way We Live," *Daily Mail*, July 6, 2010 accessed April 17, 2017, www.dailymail.co.uk/femail/article -1279906/Every-fish-knife-tells-story-BILL-BRYSON- reveals-history-homes-changed-way-live.html.

34 "Ice Creams were Produced," accessed April 18, 2017, www.monticello.org/site/jefferson/home-activity-0.

35 George Washington's Household in Philadelphia, 1790-1792, accessed April 18, 2017, www.ushistory.org/presidentshouse/history/household.php

36 Germantown's New Neighborhoods, accessed April 18, 2017, philadelphianeighborhoods.com/2010/02/03/germantowns-new-white-house/.

37 Richards, "The City Home of Benjamin Chew, Sr." 33-34, www.cliveden.org/wp-content/uploads/2013/09/Benjamin-Chew-townhouse.pdf.

38 Bulletin of the US Bureau of Labor Statistics, *History of Wages in the United States, from Colonial Times to 1928*, (October, 1929),135, accessed April 18, 2017, fraser.stlouisfed.org/files/docs/publications/bls/bls_0604_1934.pdf.

39 Richards, "The City Home of Benjamin Chew, Sr." 33 & 39, www.cliveden.org/wp-content/uploads/2013/09/Benjamin-Chew-townhouse.pdf.

40 Christopher Paul Magra, "The New England Cod Fishing Industry and Maritime Dimensions of the American Revolution" (PhD diss., University of Pittsburgh, 2006), accessed April 18, 2017, d-scholarship.pitt.edu/7982/1/Magra_ETD_1_.pdf.

41 Carson, Rachel, "Fish and Shellfish of the Middle Atlantic Coast" (1945), 16. US Fish & Wildlife Publications. Paper 3, accessed April 18, 2017, digitalcommons.unl.edu/cgi/viewcontent.cgi?article=1002&context=usfwspubs.

42 Rachel Carson, "Fish and Shellfish of the South Atlantic and Gulf Coasts" (1944), 4. US Fish & Wildlife Publications. Paper 19, accessed April 18, 2017, digitalcommons.unl.edu/cgi/viewcontent.cgi?article=1018&context=usfwspubs.

43 Andrew F. Smith, "The Food and Drink of New York," in *Gastropolis*, edited by Annie Hauck-Lawson and Jonathan Deutsch, 35-42, New York: Columbia University Press, 2008.

44 Margaret Brown Klapthor, *The First Ladies Cookbook*, (New York: Parents Magazine Press, 1969), vi.

45 Oliver, *Food in Colonial and Federal America*, 69.

46 Elizabeth Raffald, *The Experienced English House-keeper for the Use and Ease of Ladies, House-keepers, Cooks & c.* (Manchester: self-published, 1769), 319, accessed April 18, 2017, lcweb2.loc.gov/cgi-bin/displayPhoto.pl?path=/service/rbc/rbc0001/2013/2013gen60076&topImages=0332r.jpg&topLinks=0332v.jpg,0332u.tif,0332a.tif,0332.tif&displayProfile=0.

47 Oliver, Food in Colonial and Federal America, 76.

48 Oliver, Food in Colonial and Federal America, 71.

Chapter 4

49 Jim Chevallier, "Breakfast in the Eighteenth Century: The Unexamined Meal," Article on Chez Jim, accessed April 18, 2017, chezjim.com/18c/breakfast-18th.htm#_ednref64.

50 Nina York, "Our Island Still Retains a Few Danish Food Traditions," *St Croix This Week*, accessed April 18, 2017, www.stcroixthisweek.com/articles/our-island-still-retains-a-few-danish-food-traditions.html.

51 Oliver, *Food in Colonial and Federal America*, 80–85.

52 Mongin and Whidden, "Historic Structure Report: Hamilton Grange National Memorial", 50, accessed April 18, 2017, www.nps.gov/hagr/learn/historyculture/upload/Historic-Structure-Report.pdf.

53 Danielle Funiciello, Schuyler Mansion Historic Site, e-mail message to author, February 3, 2017.

54 Account with Reinhard Kahmer, October 29, 1791, Hamilton Papers, accessed April 18, 2017 founders.archives.gov/documents/Hamilton/01-09-02-0307.

55 Danielle Funiciello, Schuyler Mansion Historic Site, e-mail message to author, February 3, 2017.

56 Mongin and Whidden, "Historic Structure Report: Hamilton Grange National Memorial", Illustration

13, accessed April 18, 2017, www.nps.gov/hagr/learn/historyculture/upload/Historic-Structure-Report.pdf.

57 Oliver, *Food in Colonial and Federal America*, 161.

58 Smith, "The Food and Drink of New York," *Gastropolis*, page 36.

59 Lila Perl, Slumps, Grunts and Snickerdoodles: What Colonial America Ate and Why (New York: Clarion Books), 69, 76.

60 Laurie Kamens, "How Alexander Hamilton Did Breakfast." *Extra Crispy*, August 10, 2016, accessed April 18, 2017, www.extracrispy.com/culture/586/how-alexander-hamilton-did-breakfast.

61 Chevallier, "Breakfast in the Eighteenth Century: The Unexamined Meal," accessed April 18, 2017, chezjim.com/18c/breakfast-18th.htm#_ednref64.

62 Chernow, *Alexander Hamilton*, 205, quoting Reminiscences of James A. Hamilton.

63 Sandra L. Oliver, Food in Colonial and Federal America, 148-149.

64 Sandra L. Oliver, Food in Colonial and Federal America, 168-169.

65 Jan Whitaker, "From Patrons to Chefs, a History of Women in Restaurants," Boston Hospitality Review (August 21, 2015), accessed April 18, 2017 www.bu.edu/bhr/2015/08/21/from-patrons-to-chefs-a-history-of-women-in-restaurants/.

66 Smith, "The Food and Drink of New York," *Gastropolis*, page 44.

67 The Morris-Jumel Mansion described in *All Things Hamilton: Your Information Portal to Alexander Hamilton*, accessed April 18, 2017, allthingshamilton.com/index.php/aph-home/new-york/morris-jumel-mansion-ny.

68 Brian Levinson, "Morris-Jumel Mansion: Secrets of Manhattan's Oldest Home, in Washington Heights" www.amny.com/secrets-of-new-york/morris-jumel-mansion-secrets-of-manhattan-s-oldest-home-in-washington-heights-1.11340525.

69 James Gabler, *Dine with Thomas Jefferson and Fascinating Guests* (Palm Beach: Bacchus Press Ltd., 2015), 120–122.

70 Gabler, *Dine with Thomas Jefferson and Fascinating Guests*, 250-251 footnote 10.

71 Charles A. Cerami, *Dinner at Mr. Jefferson's* (Hoboken: John Wiley & Sons, Inc. 2008), 130–132.

72 Chernow, *Alexander Hamilton*, 616.

73 Hannah Glasse, *The Art of Cookery Made Plain and Easy*; Excelling Anything of the Kind ever yet Published. (Alexandria: Cottom and Stewart, 1805).

74 Richard Briggs, *The English Art of Cookery*, According to the Present Practice: Being a Complete Guide to all Housekeepers on a Plan Entirely New, Consisting of 28 Chapters. (London: G.G. & J. Robinson, 1794).

75 Smith, "The Food and Drink of New York," *Gastropolis*, page 44.

76 Nancy Baggett, "Ice Cream's Always Gone Over Big in Washington" *The Washington Post*, July 7, 2004; Page F06 last accessed April 18, 2017, www.washingtonpost.com/wp-dyn/articles/A30711-2004Jul6.html.

About the Author

Laura Kumin is the creator of MotherWouldKnow, a popular food blog, and is a *Huffington Post* blogger. She also teaches cooking and food history. Laura had a 20-plus year career as a lawyer before turning to food-related subjects. After keeping her research skills firmly based in legal minutiae for decades, she now gets to dig around in more fascinating territory. Her own recipe development and blogposts show a definite preference for desserts, especially chocolate ones, and fun snacks and side dishes.